Blue Collar
Food

Blue Collar Food

Easy Home Cooking for Hardworking People by Two Really Nice Guys

Chris Styler and Bill Hodge

Hearst Books / New York

Library of Congress Cataloging-in-Publication Data

Styler, Christopher.
Blue collar food : easy home cooking for hardworking
people by two really nice guys /
Chris Styler and Bill Hodge.
p.   cm.
Includes index.
ISBN 0-688-12373-2
1. Cookery.   I. Hodge, Bill.   II. Title.
TX652.S8   1994
641.5—dc20   93-41753
CIP

Printed in the United States of America

First Edition

1 2 3 4 5 6 7 8 9 10

BOOK DESIGN BY RICHARD ORIOLO

For my family, again,
and for my partner, Bill, who proved
conclusively that a friendship
can survive a partnership
and vice versa.

C.S.

To my wife, Colleen,
for her love and support throughout
the writing of this book.

B.H.

Contents

Acknowledgments

We heard horror stories of the terrible effects that co-authoring a book can have on a friendship, especially when the co-authors also happen to be the operators of a rapidly growing business who spend about twelve hours a day together. But the warnings were more terrifying than the reality: some flying skillets, a couple of flesh wounds, and some minor fractures that our doctors agree should heal normally, given time. We were helped through this last year by family, incredibly hardworking employees, and caring friends.

First, we would like to thank our crew, Fernando, Sasa, Keith, Mike, Jill, Alfonso, and Ching-Chong. Extra special thanks to Gary Maurer, without whom so much of what we have achieved in the last two years would not have been possible. For his valor in the face of midtown Manhattan traffic alone, he will always keep a special place in our hearts.

Andy Romeo gave us our first break by leasing us a corner of his kitchen, and for that we are extremely grateful.

Danny and Lois Bloom have passed much business our way, especially at the beginning when we needed it most.

Harriet Bell at William Morrow gave us the opportunity to write this book and encouraged us to make it better at every turn. We thank Harriet for her patience and support.

Susan Derescky cared for the manuscript as if it were her own. Thanks to Susan for the many hours she put in refining and focusing the recipes and the writing.

And last, but certainly not least, we would like to thank our customers, especially Howard, Jason, Talitha, and Chris; Dallas, Ronald, Nina, and Diana; Deborah W.; Johnathan and Suzanne; Kevin, Garth, and Sheila; everybody at the Joan Rivers show, the Geraldo Rivera show, the Ricki Lake show, and Bruce, Patti, and Terry.

Introduction

In 1992, after years of working in professional kitchens——make that other people's professional kitchens——we decided to get together and go into business for ourselves. We didn't know what to call our new business. Then Colleen, Bill's wife, came up with the name Blue Collar Food, and it stuck.

What the name means to us is honest food——simple foods prepared in ways people can relate to. We're a couple of down-to-earth guys ourselves, and this was to be down-to-earth foods, no difficult-to-find or expensive items, no time-consuming techniques.

Between the two of us, we have twenty-five years' combined experience cooking professionally. We've run kitchens that feed more than a thousand people a day, worked the line at the Four Seasons, trained with the last _monzù_ in Sicily, performed as fish and meat butchers, taught cooking classes, and written about food for publication. And yet, the book we set out to write together was not a collection of extravagant recipes from around the world but rather a book that would feel comfortable in the hands of the home cook.

We're home cooks too. When we come home from work, we're tired; we don't have much time or energy to prepare dinner. We both have tiny urban apartments with no specialized equipment, no restaurant range, no counter space, and, above all, no staff. But we noticed that when we cook at home, we use a simplified version of the professional techniques we've picked up over the years. We plan our dinner the same way we plan a dinner party at work—we look at how much work has to go into it, how much of that work can be done ahead, how much the food costs, how to balance nutrition, appearance, and taste. We use shortcuts and dishes that can be done ahead. We make the most of leftovers. We keep the pantry stocked. We don't fuss.

Throughout this book we've shared our experience, what we've learned from practical experience. We've explained the techniques underlying our dishes as clearly as we could because we believe that mastery of technique is the key to an increased sense of confidence and adventure in the kitchen.

We don't expect this book to change anyone's life, but we do hope it will convince you to slow down from time to time and treat yourself and those you care for to good food, lovingly prepared. Even for us, after all the years we've been cooking for a living, that is still one of life's simplest and most rewarding pleasures.

Chris Styler
Bill Hodge

Sandwiches and Starters

Blue Collar Food is a hands-on operation. We like to use our hands (washed first, of course) to toss salads, mix meat loaf, knead dough. We also like to eat with our hands. In that, we are like most Americans. Just try to find a knife and fork in a food court and you'll see what we mean.

When we do informal parties, whether buffets or barbecues, we always include some handheld starters. People seem more relaxed with chips and dips or tidbits they can pick up with their fingers than with hors d'oeuvres that have to be eaten with a fork off a plate. We've eliminated the plate hassle——how to hold your glass, how to wipe your mouth, where to put the plate down when you're finished. Life is too short for all that.

The other side of our business is wholesale, and we've built it on and around the sandwich. The sandwich is the quintessential American food—— simple, direct, and democratic. Everyone's a chief in the realm of the sandwich.

Sandwiches

When we started Blue Collar Food, we worked out of the Broadway Diner in midtown Manhattan. We kept our food in plastic milk crates, which were piled one on top of the other in a corner of their walk-in refrigerator. Whatever we needed, it seemed, was always in the bottom crate. But we had high hopes and plenty of stamina.

One day we got a call from an old friend, who had just opened an espresso bar in Greenwich Village. "Do you do sandwiches?" he wanted to know. We hadn't thought of that, but we said yes. When you're working out of a plastic crate in someone else's refrigerator, you always say yes. "Can you bring me some samples?" he said. "Today." When you're running an espresso bar, you always say today.

We threw together about ten different sandwiches, grabbing whatever we could lay our hands on—bread here, fillings there—wrapped them nicely and arranged them in a basket. Even among friends, you think of looks when you're trying to make a sale. We took a cab downtown and left off the samples and a price list. We'd barely gotten back when he was on the phone with his order: Six dozen sandwiches. Tomorrow.

It was crazy—the bakery didn't have the same breads, we'd used up all our supplies—but somehow we made it. There's been no turning back. Our friend's place was the first of many espresso bars to open in New York. Every week we'd rush out to get *New York* magazine and the food section of *The New York Times* to check the listings. We'd fill a crate with sandwich fixings, get in Bill's beat-up old BMW with Bill behind the wheel and Chris in the passenger seat making sandwiches on his knees as we raced to beat out the competition with our sandwiches.

Soon we added soup and desserts to our wholesale menu, but we've always credited sandwiches with putting us on the map. We've included some typical ones in this chapter, but there are others in the book. Our nostalgic cream cheese on Date Nut Bread (page 242) and the vegetarian Hummus (page 36) on pumpernickel are both best-sellers. We often recycle leftovers into sandwiches. Turkey Meat Loaf (page 148) on rye, for example, is great. Our multiethnic mozzarella and tomato on a sesame seed bagel seemed too simple to write up as a recipe.

Actually, we believe the best sandwiches, like Dagwood Bumstead's skyscraping creations, are the product of innovation. Everyone knows how to make a sandwich; inspiration determines what goes in it. From the ultimate in luxury, like our friend Brendan Walsh's lobster and avocado on roasted pepper brioche, to the simplest po'boy, sandwiches offer more creative possibilities than any other type of food. They can be any size or shape, hot or cold, sweet or spicy, rustic or elegant. Best of all, a sandwich can be eaten any time of day or night.

So next time you think there's nothing to eat in the house, look around. You've probably got some crackers or English muffins, a can of tuna or sardines, a couple of eggs in the fridge, lettuce, a pepper in the crisper. Think creatively. Remember, you're making a sandwich, not a statement.

Curried Tuna on Dark Bread

Makes 4 sandwiches

Colleen, Bill's wife, adds a small amount of curry powder to her salad dressing for extra zip. We carried the idea a step further and developed a curried tuna salad that tastes as great as it looks, especially when piled on pumpernickel bread and topped with alfalfa sprouts or a few thin cucumber slices. Cooking the curry powder in a little oil releases its flavors.

Two 6⅛-ounce cans chunk white tuna in water

2 teaspoons vegetable oil

1 teaspoon curry powder

5 tablespoons mayonnaise

2 teaspoons fresh lemon juice

2 tablespoons very finely diced red onion

1 small carrot, peeled and grated

Freshly ground black pepper

8 slices pumpernickel bread

Alfalfa sprouts (optional)

Cucumber slices (optional)

1. Drain the tuna in a sieve and press lightly to squeeze out as much liquid as possible. Set aside.

2. Heat the vegetable oil and curry powder in small skillet over medium heat just until the curry powder begins to sizzle, about 1 minute. Or stir the curry powder and oil together in a small microwave-safe bowl. Cook on high for 1 minute. Transfer the curry mixture to a small bowl and stir in the mayonnaise and lemon juice. Add the onion, carrot, pepper, and tuna. Mix well until thoroughly blended. *The salad may be prepared completely up to 2 days in advance.*

3. Divide the tuna salad among 4 slices of the bread. Top with sprouts or cucumber, if desired. Close the sandwiches, pressing lightly to help them hold together. Cut in half and serve.

Smoked Salmon and Cucumber Sandwich

Makes 2 sandwiches

Smoked salmon is a luxury we all need to indulge ourselves in from time to time. This delicate sandwich makes the most of it.

4 thin slices dark pumpernickel or dark rye bread (see Note)
2 tablespoons Grainy Mustard Mayonnaise (page 29)
16 very thin slices cucumber
2 ounces good-quality smoked salmon, thinly sliced
Small sprigs watercress (optional)

Spread 1 side of each of the slices of bread with the mustard mayonnaise. Arrange the cucumber in an even layer over two of the slices. Top the cucumber with an even layer of smoked salmon and the watercress, if you like. Close the sandwiches and press them lightly but firmly to help them hold together. Cut the sandwiches in four from corner to corner.

Note: What we have in mind is a kind of Central European bread that is square, dense, and intense in flavor; it comes very thinly sliced. Look for cellophane- or foil-wrapped loaves about four inches square at the deli counter of your supermarket.

Pecan-Orange-Chicken Salad Sandwich

Makes 6 sandwiches

Don't knock it till you try it. The combination sounds odd, we know, but we also know you're going to like it. Since the salad gets better as it stands, it's a perfect choice to make ahead.

2 navel oranges

4 cups diced roasted chicken (see Note)

¼ cup toasted chopped pecans (see Note)

1 small red onion, finely diced

½ cup mayonnaise

1 tablespoon balsamic vinegar

½ teaspoon kosher salt

¼ teaspoon freshly ground black pepper

1 teaspoon chopped fresh sage (optional)

12 slices whole wheat or *pain de campagne*

1. Using a fine grater, remove enough of the zest from the oranges to measure 1 teaspoon. Be sure not to grate into the bitter white pith under the zest. Place the zest in a large bowl. Cut away the remaining peel and the pith from the oranges. Working over the bowl, cut out the individual orange segments and let them drop into the bowl. After you've cut out all the segments squeeze out the juice from the membrane into the bowl.

2. Add the chicken, pecans, onion, mayonnaise, vinegar, salt, pepper, and sage, if desired. Toss gently until well blended. Taste and adjust the seasoning. Cover and refrigerate until ready to serve. *The salad can be prepared entirely up to 2 days in advance and refrigerated. Bring the salad to room temperature and check the seasoning before serving.*

3. Divide the salad among 6 slices of bread. Cover with the remaining bread, pressing to help the sandwiches hold together. Cut in half and serve.

Notes: A 3½-pound chicken will yield about 4 cups of diced meat. Either roast your own chicken (page 154) or buy a rotisserie chicken. Let the meat cool to room temperature before adding it to the salad.

Toast the pecans in a small skillet over medium-low heat, shaking the pan frequently, until golden brown, about 3 minutes. Remove from the pan. Let the nuts cool to room temperature before adding them to the salad.

Oriental sesame oil, the dark brown kind, gives you a big bang for your buck. We use it here to flavor a light salad. A few drops will also do wonders for salad dressing and add oomph to grilled chicken or fish. This sandwich filling, whether made with shrimp or chicken, can also be served as a light first course.

16 medium (26 to 30 per pound) shrimp, peeled, deveined, and cooked (page 41)

½ cup very thinly sliced red cabbage or radicchio

½ pound loose or half 10-ounce cellophane pack fresh spinach leaves, stemmed, washed, and drained (4 cups)

¼ cup toasted pine nuts or slivered almonds (see Note)

2 tablespoons fresh lemon juice

1 tablespoon oriental sesame oil

½ teaspoon kosher salt

2 large pita breads, whole wheat or white

1. Combine the shrimp, cabbage, spinach, and pine nuts in a large mixing bowl. Sprinkle with the lemon juice, sesame oil, and salt. Toss until the ingredients are coated with the dressing.

2. Cut the pita breads in half crosswise to make pockets. Divide the mixture among the pockets. Serve at once.

Note: Toast the nuts in a small skillet over medium-low heat, stirring frequently, until they turn golden brown, about 3 minutes. Remove from the pan immediately and let cool.

Substitute ¾ pound skinless and boneless chicken breast for the shrimp. Poach or grill the chicken breast, dice it, and let cool to room temperature before adding to the salad.

Santa Fe Chicken Melt

Makes 2 sandwiches

We are constantly looking for new ideas for grilled sandwiches. Everyone loves them. This one is filled with the flavors of the American Southwest, which are as much at home in the Northeast these days. Let us assure you, you don't have to train as a short-order cook in a lunch wagon to make a good grilled sandwich. Just use a griddle or heavy skillet and weight the sandwich while it grills.

10 ounces skinless and boneless chicken breast

4 teaspoons vegetable oil

1 teaspoon chili powder

1 teaspoon kosher salt

4 slices dense-textured white or wheat bread or two 5-inch lengths
   Italian bread (see Note)

2 tablespoons Salsa Mayonnaise (page 29)

Shredded iceberg lettuce (optional)

2 ounces jack cheese, thinly sliced (about 6 slices)

1 tablespoon unsalted butter

1. Trim all fat from the chicken. If necessary, cut into single breasts. Stir 2 teaspoons of the oil, the chili powder, and salt together in a mixing bowl. Add the chicken breasts, one at a time, and turn until they are coated with marinade. Cover the bowl and refrigerate the chicken breasts for up to 1 day.

2. Set up the grill, light the coals, and place the grill 4 inches above them. When the coals are ready, grill the chicken breast about 4 inches from the heat until cooked through, but still moist, 10 minutes or less, depending on how thick it is. Move and turn the chicken several times during cooking. Or broil the chicken about 4 inches from the heat, turning and moving it several times, until done, about 10 minutes. Remove and let stand at room temperature for at least 15 minutes before slicing.

3.   Spread 1 side of each piece of bread or the insides of the Italian bread with the salsa mayonnaise. Cover 2 pieces of the bread with shredded lettuce, if desired. Slice the chicken breasts very thin on an angle and divide evenly between 2 slices of the bread, making an even layer on each. Cover the chicken with cheese. Place the other slice of bread on top, dry side up. Press the sandwiches firmly to help them hold together during cooking. *The sandwiches can be made to this point up to 4 hours in advance. Cover in plastic wrap and refrigerate. Remove from the refrigerator and bring to room temperature 30 minutes before grilling.*

4.   Heat the remaining vegetable oil and the butter on a griddle over medium-low heat. When the butter just begins to brown, place the sandwiches on the griddle and weight them. Cook until the underside is crisp and golden brown, about 5 minutes. Flip the sandwiches and cook until the second side is crisp and golden and the filling is warmed through, about 4 minutes. Remove and let stand for 1 minute. Cut in half and serve.

Notes: If you are using Italian bread, cut a very thin sliver from the top (rounded) crust to help the sandwich lie flat during cooking. Cut the bread in half lengthwise.

Weight the sandwiches with a professional bacon press (a piece of heavy metal with a wooden handle). Lacking a press, place a saucer on top of the sandwich and a heavy can on top of that.

Cuban Sandwich

Makes 2 sandwiches

In the years after Fidel Castro came to power in Havana, Cuban refugees took over scores of coffee shops and luncheonettes in New York City and transformed them into Cuban and Cuban-Chinese restaurants, which thrived on the isle of Manhattan. Many have folded in recent years—our favorite was replaced not long ago by a fast-food operation—but the Cuban, a grilled pork sandwich, lives on. Fans of the Cuban can argue at length over what goes in it and where to get the best one. The kosher dill pickle is a typical New York ethnic crossover.

Two 5-inch lengths Italian bread
½ kosher dill pickle, thinly sliced
2 ounces thinly sliced Swiss cheese (see Note)
2 ounces thinly sliced boiled or baked ham
¼ pound thinly sliced roast pork
1 tablespoon vegetable oil
1 tablespoon unsalted butter

1. Cut a very thin sliver from the top (rounded) crust to help the sandwiches lie flat during cooking. Cut each length of the bread in half lengthwise. Arrange the pickle slices overlapping down 1 side of the bread. Arrange the cheese in an even layer on the other side. Arrange the ham and pork over the cheese in an even layer. Close the sandwiches. *The sandwiches can be made to this point up to 4 hours in advance. Cover in plastic wrap and refrigerate. Remove from the refrigerator and let stand at room temperature 30 minutes before grilling.*

2. Heat the vegetable oil and the butter on a griddle over medium-low heat. When the butter just begins to brown, place the sandwich on the griddle and weight them if you like. Cook until the underside is crisp and golden brown, about 5 minutes. Flip the sandwiches and cook until the second side is crisp and golden and the cheese is melted, about 4 minutes. Remove and let stand for 1 minute. Cut in half and serve.

Note: It is difficult to give amounts other than weights for the meats and cheeses that go into this sandwich. There should be enough ham and cheese to make a thin, even layer of each and about twice as much roast pork. Exact amounts actually aren't important. You'll probably find yourself altering the proportions to suit your own taste.

Blue Collar Barbecued Beef Sandwich

Makes 4 sandwiches

We pride ourselves on finding creative ways to use leftovers. We often cook more roast beef or pork than we can use at once; when that happens, we turn the ends into a sandwich filling like this one. The pickled onions are a must. And remember: Haute couture may go with haute cuisine, but old shirts go best with sloppy sandwiches.

1 pound cooked roast beef or roast pork

1 cup Blue Collar's 1-2-3 BBQ Sauce (page 45) or bottled barbecue
  sauce

4 kaiser rolls, hero rolls, or four 5-inch lengths Italian bread

½ cup Pickled Red Onions (page 29)

Hot pepper sauce (optional)

1. Cut the beef into ½-inch dice. Pulse the beef, a third at a time, in the food processor. Pulse once or twice, just until the beef is coarsely shredded or chopped. Repeat with the remaining beef.

2. Combine the beef and barbecue sauce in a mixing bowl and stir until blended. Cut the rolls open, leaving each one joined along 1 side. Either serve the barbecued beef at room temperature or warm it over low heat until simmering. Divide the beef among the rolls and top each with some pickled onions. Pass hot pepper sauce separately, if desired.

Sandwich Breads

Any kind of bread is good for a sandwich, from crackers to walnut or olive bread from the latest chi-chi bakery. We think it's a good idea to keep a box of crackers or flat bread like matzo or lavash in the cupboard and English muffins, bagels (cut them in half first), pita bread, and tortillas in the freezer.

Bakery breads make more interesting sandwiches than packaged bread. It's hard to be specific since bread availability varies so much across the country, but we consider the following to be among the best choices: Jewish rye, with or without seeds, or pumpernickel; French or Italian long loaves; semolina bread; rustic breads like *pain de campagne* or *pain au levain;* six-grain bread. Fresh rolls we've found to be good for sandwiches include kaiser rolls, club rolls, and onion rolls. We also like packaged square pumpernickel and dark rye.

In the worst-case scenario, in which you've rented a cabin on a pristine lake, but the nearest supermarket stocks only packaged bread, buy familiar premium brands. Bread is not like beer, where local breweries often supply a better and cheaper product than the big boys. If there's an oven in the cabin, consider frozen pizza shells. You're on vacation. Have a beer. Go fishing.

Focaccia Pizza

Makes 8 servings

Half American Pizza with the Works and half Sicilian sfincione, this hybrid is a surefire crowd pleaser. Add to the toppings whatever you fancy: black olives, anchovies, strips of hot cherry peppers, dried oregano, fresh basil. Cut this thick-crust pizza into pieces any size you want——smaller for party tidbits, larger for bigger appetites.

Focaccia dough (page 20), made with or without dried herbs

2 cups sliced mushrooms, sliced red onion, thin strips of red, yellow, or green bell peppers, or any combination

2 tablespoons olive oil

¾ cup Tomato Sauce, preferably homemade (page 95) or 2 ripe medium tomatoes, cored and thinly sliced

2 cups grated mozzarella, gruyère, or muenster, or any combination

¼ cup grated parmesan or romano

1. Make the dough through Step 3.

2. Turn the dough out onto a work surface and pound it once or twice to deflate it. Transfer the dough to a lightly oiled 16 × 11-inch baking sheet or jelly-roll pan. Stretch the dough with your fingertips to form an even layer that covers the bottom of the pan completely. The dough will want to shrink back to its original size. Do your best. Let the dough rest for 10 minutes before finishing.

3. Toss the vegetables in a bowl with the oil. Finish stretching the dough. Cover the top with an even layer of sauce or sliced tomatoes. Spread the vegetables over that, making sure that each layer of ingredients you add goes all the way to the edges of the dough. Sprinkle the grated mozzarella over the vegetables. Sprinkle with parmesan.

4. Heat the oven to 375°F. Cover the dough lightly with a clean kitchen towel and let it rise in a warm place until the edges have swelled and are soft to the touch, about 30 to 45 minutes.

5. Bake the pizza until the underside is deep golden brown and crispy and the cheese is browned, about 35 minutes. Let cool in the pan for at least 5 minutes before serving. Slide the pizza out onto a cutting surface and cut it into serving pieces by using a downward rather than a sawing motion.

Focaccia

Makes one 9-inch focaccia

Focaccia is an Italian flat bread that's very easy to make and serves many useful purposes. We flavor ours with olive oil and herbs and use it for pizza and Calzones and as sandwich bread. We split it apart and fill it—in summer with sliced tomatoes and mozzarella moistened with a little olive oil, in winter with mortadella and provolone cheese with grainy mustard. It's also great cut in hunks to eat with grilled foods and soups.

Leftover focaccia may be thinly sliced, brushed with olive oil, and grilled or roasted until crisp. These focaccia toasts are wonderful with soups and salads.

To make sandwiches from the focaccia: First cut the focaccia into four wedges. Split each wedge and add the filling of your choice.

1 cup warm water
1 envelope dry yeast
About ⅓ cup olive oil
4 cups all-purpose flour
About 2 teaspoons kosher salt
1 teaspoon dried oregano
1 teaspoon dried basil
½ teaspoon dried rosemary

1. Stir together the water, yeast, and 4 tablespoons of the olive oil in a small bowl until the yeast is dissolved. Let stand for 5 minutes.

2. Combine 3 cups of the flour, the salt, oregano, basil, and rosemary in the workbowl of a food processor. Pour in the yeast mixture and process until the mixture forms a ball. Continue processing for 20 seconds. Or combine the flour, salt, and herbs in a large bowl and stir to mix. Make a well in the center of the flour mixture. Add the yeast mixture and stir to form a rough dough. Turn the ball of dough out onto a lightly floured surface and knead, adding flour as necessary, until the dough is very elastic and no longer sticky. If you prepared the dough by hand, this will take several minutes.

3. Place the dough in a lightly oiled bowl and turn it to coat all sides. Cover the bowl tightly with plastic wrap and place it in a warm place to rise.

4. When the dough has doubled, about 1 hour, turn it out onto a work surface. Punch the dough into a rough circle, about 9 inches across. Oil a 9-inch round pan with about 1 tablespoon olive oil and place the dough in the pan. Press the dough to the edges of the pan using your fingertips. (The little indentations made by your fingers are characteristic of focaccia.) Brush the dough with additional olive oil and sprinkle it with salt if you like. Cover the pan tightly with plastic wrap and let rise again until almost doubled in bulk. This can take from 30 minutes to 1½ hours, depending on the conditions.

5. Heat the oven to 375°F. Uncover the pan and bake the focaccia until golden brown, about 40 minutes. Let it cool in the pan for 10 minutes. Transfer it to a cooling rack.

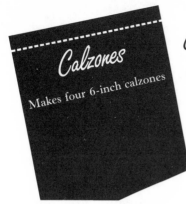

Calzones

Makes four 6-inch calzones

Calzones are a kind of inside-out pizza, with the filling enclosed in the dough instead of sitting on top of it. Italian in origin, they became a popular street food in New York and other big cities when pizza parlor operators saw the virtues of expanding beyond pizza by the pie or slice.

Focaccia dough (page 20), made with or without dried herbs

One 15-ounce container ricotta cheese

1 cup grated mozzarella, preferably fresh

¼ cup grated parmesan

1 teaspoon freshly ground black pepper

Kosher salt (optional)

1 cup Tomato Sauce, preferably homemade (page 95), or 12 thin slices
    ham (optional)

1.   Make the dough through Step 3.

2.   Combine the ricotta, mozzarella, parmesan, and black pepper in a bowl and beat until blended. Taste the mixture and add salt, if desired.

3.   Divide the dough into 4 equal parts. Roll each out on a lightly floured surface to an 8-inch circle. Sprinkle the top of each circle lightly with flour. Place a fourth of the ricotta mixture in the center of each circle. Top with tomato sauce or ham slices, if desired. Fold the dough over the filling so the edges meet and form a half moon. Pinch the edges together very firmly to seal in the filling. Place the calzones on a lightly oiled baking sheet, leaving at least 2 inches between them. Cover with a clean towel and let stand in a warm place until very soft to the touch, about 45 minutes.

4. Heat the oven to 375°F.

5. Poke the top of each calzone once or twice with a fork. Bake until golden brown, about 30 minutes. The calzones should sound hollow when tapped. Cool for at least 10 to 15 minutes before serving.

Variations

Add some cooked spinach or Swiss chard to the filling; chop it and squeeze out as much liquid as you can.

Add a few sautéed mushrooms (page 197) to the filling; drain first on paper towels.

Add 1 to 2 tablespoons chopped fresh herbs—Italian parsley is nice—to the filling.

Red Onion Bread

Makes 6 servings

We started doing this bread and the walnut-basil one that follows as a way to tart up less-than-great Italian bread. We've since found that people really like these seasoned breads. So now, even though we can and do find good bread around, we still put some of these out in baskets when we do a party. They're gone lickety-split.

1 loaf good-quality Italian bread, about 12 inches long

2 tablespoons olive oil

2 tablespoons grated parmesan or romano

1 medium red onion, peeled and very thinly sliced

1 teaspoon balsamic vinegar

1 teaspoon kosher salt

Freshly ground black pepper

1. Split the bread lengthwise. Mix the oil, parmesan, onion, vinegar, and salt in a small bowl until the onions are separated and coated with the remaining ingredients. Divide the onion mixture between the 2 pieces of bread, evenly coating both cut surfaces. Sprinkle generously with pepper. *The bread may be prepared to this point up to 8 hours in advance.* Wrap in plastic wrap and refrigerate until needed.

2. Place the oven rack in the top position and heat the oven to 375°F.

3. Place the bread on a baking sheet and bake until the underside is crisp and the onions are starting to brown, about 10 minutes. If the bread is crisp before the onions are brown, place the bread under the broiler for 1 to 2 minutes to finish browning the onions. Let stand for 1 or 2 minutes. Cut crosswise into 2-inch slices.

Walnut-Basil Bread

Makes 6 servings

The spread for this bread is similar to pesto but richer in walnuts and minus the garlic. The bread is particularly good with soup. If you have a little pesto in the fridge, you could use that for a solo portion. It won't taste quite the same, but it will give you the idea.

¼ cup olive oil

⅓ cup (packed) fresh basil leaves

¼ cup walnut pieces

About 2 tablespoons grated parmesan

½ teaspoon kosher salt

1 loaf Italian bread, about 12 inches long

1. Pour the olive oil in a blender jar and place the basil leaves on top of it. Blend at medium speed until the basil is coarsely chopped. Add the walnuts, 2 tablespoons of the parmesan, and the salt. Blend until the mixture forms a smooth paste. Stop the blender once or twice to scrape down the sides of the jar with a rubber spatula. *The paste may be prepared to this point up to 2 days in advance and refrigerated, tightly covered.*

2. Heat the oven to 375°F.

3. Split the bread lengthwise and spread both cut sides evenly with the basil mixture. Sprinkle with additional parmesan, if desired. Bake the bread directly on the oven rack until the top is lightly browned and the bottom is crisp, about 12 minutes. Remove, cut into slices, and serve hot.

Black Bean Burritos

Makes 6 servings

Chris tested this recipe at his summer house on a crowd who'd just spent the day working up a formidable appetite by lying on the beach. Not only was the food appreciated, people enjoyed hanging around the grill, warming tortillas and grilling their own chicken and shrimp. This recipe makes enough black-bean filling for six burritos (enough for six people if you're serving side dishes). Double or triple it if you're feeding a larger crowd. Set up a burritos bar with toppings and black-bean filling. Throw together a California-style avocado garnish and put that out too. Warm the tortillas on the grill or in the oven and grill or broil the chicken and shrimp as you go along.

Two 19-ounce cans black beans, rinsed and drained

¼ cup finely chopped red onion

1 jalapeño, cored and finely chopped

1 teaspoon kosher salt

2 tablespoons fresh lime juice

Iceberg lettuce, shredded

Tomato, cored, seeded, and diced

Red onion, finely diced

Jalapeño, thinly sliced

Lime wedges

Sour cream

Chicken breast (optional, see Variation)

Shrimp (optional, see Variation)

Six 12-inch flour tortillas

1. Combine the beans, chopped red onion, chopped jalapeño, salt, and lime juice in a small heavy saucepan. Heat to simmering over low heat. Simmer for 10 minutes, covered, stirring once or twice. Check the seasoning and remove from the heat. *The bean filling may be prepared to this point up to 1 day in advance. Cool the beans to room temperature and refrigerate, covered. Reheat over low heat, adding a small amount of water if necessary to restore them to a cream consistency.*

2. Prepare as many of the toppings (lettuce, tomato, onion, jalapeño, lime, and sour cream) as you like. *Toppings may be prepared to this point up to 6 hours in advance. Refrigerate the toppings, stored separately in bowls, until needed.*

3. Set up the grill, light the coals, and place the grill 4 inches above them. When the coals are ready, grill the chicken or shrimp, if using. Remove to a cutting board and let stand while preparing the tortillas. Grill the tortillas, turning once, until heated through and just a few brown spots appear, about 30 seconds to 1 minute. Transfer the tortillas to a plate and keep them warm under a clean towel.

4. Slice the chicken thin and cut the shrimp in half. Spread some of the bean filling over the center of a tortilla. Top with chicken, shrimp, or avocado and sprouts. Sprinkle the toppings of choice over the filling. Roll the burrito and eat out of hand or with a knife and fork if you prefer.

Variations

California Burritos: Peel and thinly slice a ripe avocado, preferably Haas, and toss with ½ cup alfalfa sprouts in a serving bowl. Use some to top the black-bean filling in Step 3. Makes enough for six burritos.

Chicken Burritos: Sprinkle 1 pound skinless and boneless chicken breasts with ½ teaspoon kosher salt. Coat with 1½ teaspoons Chili Rub (page 137) or 1 tablespoon olive oil. Cover and refrigerate until ready to grill, up to 1 day. Grill as described on page 26. Let stand for 5 minutes. Thinly slice and use to top the black-bean filling in Step 3. Makes enough for six burritos.

(continued)

Shrimp Burritos: Peel and devein ¾ pound medium (26 to 30 per pound) shrimp as described on page 41. Toss with ½ teaspoon kosher salt and 1 teaspoon Chili Rub (page 137) or 1 tablespoon olive oil. Cover and refrigerate until ready to grill, up to 1 day. Grill as described on page 26. Cut in half and use to top the black-bean filling in Step 3. Makes enough for six burritos.

Sandwich Enhancers

An ordinary sandwich can be transfigured by one of these simple potions. Spread a dab on the bread or, in the case of the onions, pile them on top of the filling and let the magic happen.

Salsa Mayonnaise

Leftover Salsa Cruda (page 31) becomes soggy and is not much good for dipping; however, it makes a great sandwich condiment. Drain the salsa and reserve the liquid for another use. Stir ⅓ cup salsa into 1 cup mayonnaise. Taste and add more salsa, if desired. *May be stored, covered, in the refrigerator for up to 3 days.*

Grainy Mustard Mayonnaise

Stir equal amounts of prepared mayonnaise and grainy mustard in a small bowl until thoroughly blended. *May be stored, covered, in the refrigerator for up to 1 month.*

Honey Mustard Glaze

Stir 2 tablespoons honey into 1 cup mild Dijon mustard. *May be stored, covered, in the refrigerator for up to 1 month.*

Horseradish-Dill Mustard

Stir 1 tablespoon horseradish and 1 tablespoon chopped fresh dill into 1 cup mild Dijon mustard. *May be stored, covered, in the refrigerator for up to 1 month.*

Pickled Red Onions

Peel 2 medium red onions (about ½ pound) and slice them about ¼ inch thick. Bring ½ cup white wine vinegar, ⅓ cup sugar, and 1 teaspoon kosher salt to a boil in a small saucepan. Stir in the onions, cover the pan, and boil until the onions are softened, about 3 minutes. Remove from the heat and cool completely. Makes 1 cup. *May be stored, covered, in the refrigerator for up to 1 week.*

Starters

When we cater a party, we always come prepared with starters, little snacks that fill the gap until it's time to really eat. We've found people arrive at a party in full appetite. None of that quaint antebellum custom of eating *before* the ball.

For the most part, we like starters that can be put around the room or deck so that people feel encouraged to circulate. At barbecues, we like the idea of giving a foretaste of what's to come. We've also found that people tend to congregate around the grill and kibbitz. So we hand them a grilled shrimp or chicken wing and send them on their way.

The dishes in this section are stand-up starters. More formal first courses are scattered throughout the book, in the chapters on vegetables, soups, salads, and pasta.

Salsa Cruda

Makes 2 cups

We find people love chips and dips, and we usually provide several for casual parties. Simple as salsa is, it's always popular, maybe because it's so light and refreshing. You can also spoon salsa over grilled chicken or fish. Use the excess liquid to season soup or salad dressing. Or go Blue Collar frugal and stir it into a Bloody Mary made with tequila instead of vodka. Waste not, want not.

1 ripe large tomato, cored and cut into ¼-inch dice
¼ cup very finely diced red onion
1 tablespoon chopped fresh cilantro
1 jalapeño, cored, seeded, and finely chopped
Kosher salt
Fresh lime juice (optional)

Combine the tomato, onion, cilantro, and jalapeño in a bowl and toss to mix. Add salt to taste and lime juice, if desired. Let the salsa stand for 10 minutes, drain the liquid, and check again for seasoning just before serving.

Note: To save on last-minute preparation, cut up all the ingredients a day ahead, refrigerate them separately, and mix shortly before serving.

Crostini with Tomato-Basil Topping

Makes 4 servings

Crostini, Italian for little toasts (they used to be called <u>tartines</u> when French was in fashion), are among the most versatile of starters since almost anything can serve as a topping. For formal parties with passed hors d'oeuvres, we make a variety of toppings—pesto, roasted peppers, green olive paste, and fresh mozzarella, in addition to the ones in this recipe— and arrange each tray with an assortment of crostini, no two alike.

We also like the idea of a self-serve crostini bar: Set out a basket of crostini and surround it with bowls of topping. Let guests help themselves.

Sixteen ½-inch slices Italian or French bread (see Note)

Olive oil

2 ripe medium tomatoes, seeded and diced (about 1½ cups)

2 tablespoons olive oil

2 tablespoons chopped fresh basil

1 teaspoon wine vinegar

Kosher salt

Freshly ground black pepper

1. Heat the oven to 350°F.

2. Lightly brush both sides of each slice of bread with oil. Arrange the bread on a baking sheet and bake until golden brown and crisp, about 12 minutes. Remove and cool. *Crostini may be prepared to this point up to 2 days in advance. Store them in a tightly covered container at room temperature.*

3. Combine the tomatoes, oil, basil, vinegar, and salt and pepper to taste in a bowl. Toss to mix and let stand for 10 to 15 minutes.

4. Spoon some of the tomatoes on top of each of the toasts or serve the topping and toasts separately for guests to serve themselves.

Note: For best results, the bread should be about 3 inches wide in the middle; the lighter the texture, the crisper the crostini. You can also use whole wheat or semolina bread for crostini.

Variations

Prosciutto-Parmesan Topping: Using a vegetable peeler, shave a ¼-pound piece of parmesan into 1 cup of thin curls. Cut 4 to 6 thin slices of prosciutto (about 2 ounces) into thin strips. Separate the strips and toss with the parmesan, about 1 tablespoon olive oil, and a generous amount of freshly ground black pepper. Makes enough for 16 crostini.

Smoked Salmon Topping: Beat ¼ cup sour cream, 1 tablespoon chopped chives (fresh or dried), and a generous amount of freshly ground black pepper in a bowl until blended. Spread on crostini and top with thin slices of smoked salmon (you will need about 2 ounces). Garnish with more chives, if desired. Makes enough for 16 crostini.

White Bean Topping: Mash 1 cup of rinsed and drained canned white beans with 2 tablespoons olive oil, 1 teaspoon lemon juice, and a generous amount of freshly ground black pepper. Add 1 tablespoon chopped fresh parsley, if desired. Makes enough for 16 crostini.

Guacamole

Makes 2 cups

Two things to remember when making guacamole: One, think ahead since it's difficult if not impossible to buy ripe avocados when you need them. Two, stop mashing before the guacamole gets smooth. One of us (Bill) mashes his avocado with a fork; the other (Chris) cuts his into large dice that break down when mixed. Such is the strength of our relationship that we've been able to overcome monumental differences like this. We suggest you try both ways and see which you prefer. We agree, though, that guacamole is best made with the pebbly skinned California avocado, especially the black Haas, rather than that bright green dinosaur egg of an avocado from Florida.

2 ripe but firm medium avocados, preferably Haas
2 tablespoons lime juice
½ small red onion, minced
1 ripe plum tomato, cored, seeded, and chopped
1 jalapeño pepper, cored, seeded, and finely diced
1 tablespoon chopped fresh cilantro
Kosher salt
Freshly ground black pepper

Peel the avocados and cut away the flesh from the pit. Either dice the avocado or mash it coarsely with a fork. Immediately place the avocado in a bowl and stir in the lime juice until the avocado is coated. Stir in the onion, tomato, jalapeño, cilantro, and salt and pepper to taste. Let the guacamole stand at room temperature for about 30 minutes before serving. *Guacamole is best served within the hour, but it can be refrigerated for up to 4 hours. Refrigerate the guacamole in a serving bowl with a piece of plastic wrap pressed against the surface to prevent browning.*

Black Bean Dip

Makes 4 cups

When we do a barbecue, we set a pot of this dip on the side of the grill to keep warm, scooping it out into smaller bowls as needed. Toasted yellow and blue corn chips are the instruments of choice for dipping.

1¼ cups black beans (½ pound)

½ cup sour cream

½ cup diced roasted red pepper

2 scallions, thinly sliced

2 tablespoons chopped fresh cilantro

1½ tablespoons fresh lime juice

Kosher salt

Freshly ground black pepper

1. Soak and cook the beans as described on page 212.

2. Set aside ½ cup of the cooking liquid and drain the beans thoroughly. Combine ½ cup of the cooked beans and the reserved cooking liquid in a food processor or blender and process until smooth. Transfer the bean puree to a bowl and stir in the remaining beans, the sour cream, roasted pepper, scallions, cilantro, and lime juice. Add salt and pepper to taste. *The dip may be prepared up to 1 day in advance. Refrigerate, covered, and bring to room temperature for 1 hour before serving.*

Hummus

Makes 1¼ cups

Thanks to the food processor, hummus, which once had to be beaten interminably with a wooden spoon, can be made without a workout. And thanks to canned chick peas, it can be made in less than a quarter of an hour. Serve it with toasted pita chips as a dip or on pumpernickel bread with sliced cucumber, tomato, and sprouts as a sandwich. The latter is a big seller in Greenwich Village espresso bars.

One 15½-ounce can chick peas, rinsed and drained
1 tablespoon fresh lemon juice
2 teaspoons oriental sesame oil
1 clove garlic, minced
3 tablespoons olive oil
¼ cup minced parsley
3 scallions, thinly sliced
Kosher salt
Freshly ground black pepper
Toasted pita chips (see Note)

1. Process the chick peas, lemon juice, sesame oil, and garlic in a food processor until the chick peas are finely chopped. Add the olive oil slowly with the motor running and process until the hummus is the consistency of a coarse puree.

2. Transfer the hummus to a bowl and stir in the parsley, scallions, and salt and pepper to taste. Hummus may be refrigerated, covered, for up to 3 days. Bring the hummus to room temperature about 30 minutes before serving.

Note: To make toasted pita chips, split a pita bread, preferably whole wheat, into top and bottom rounds. Cut each round into 8 wedges and brush both sides of each wedge very lightly with olive or peanut oil. Toast the wedges on a baking sheet in a 350°F. oven until crisp, about 10 minutes. Cool before serving.

Baked Herbed Brie with Crumb Crust

Makes 6 servings

This recipe makes a perfect party appetizer or hors d'oeuvre before guests come to the table. It can even stand duty as a first course—alone or atop a salad of mixed greens.

1 egg

1 tablespoon Dijon mustard

¼ teaspoon kosher salt

Pinch freshly ground black pepper

½ cup all-purpose flour

1 cup dried breadcrumbs

One 12-ounce wheel herbed brie

1. Beat the egg, mustard, salt, and pepper with a few drops of water in a shallow bowl until thoroughly blended. Spread out the flour and breadcrumbs on separate plates or sheets of wax paper. Roll the brie in the flour until all sides are coated. Tap off any excess. Coat the brie in the egg mixture, letting any excess drip off, then in the breadcrumbs, pressing gently so they stick to the surface. *The cheese may be prepared to this point up to 1 day in advance.*

2. Heat the oven to 375°F.

3. Bake the brie on a lightly oiled sheet pan until the crumbs are golden brown, about 10 minutes. Serve immediately.

Broiled Marinated Mushrooms

Makes 4 servings

Here's a great way to dress up plain mushrooms. Use any size you want, depending on how you want to serve them—tiny to spear with toothpicks, medium for a platter of broiled vegetables or antipasto, large to accompany grilled meat or poultry, jumbo for a first course.

1½ pounds button mushrooms
4 tablespoons olive oil
2 tablespoons fresh lemon juice
1 teaspoon dried tarragon
½ teaspoon kosher salt
Freshly ground black pepper
2 tablespoons chopped fresh parsley

1. Wipe the mushrooms clean with a paper towel or the palm of your hand and place them in a large bowl. Slowly pour 3 tablespoons of the olive oil over them while tossing. Add the lemon juice, tarragon, salt, and pepper to taste. Toss to mix.

2. Arrange the mushrooms in a single layer on a broiler pan. Broil about 4 inches from the heat until they begin to brown, about 3 minutes. Turn the mushrooms and continue broiling until lightly browned on all sides, about 4 minutes.

3. Transfer the mushrooms and any juice in the pan to a bowl. Let stand for 5 minutes. Drain off all but 2 tablespoons of the juice. Add the remaining 1 tablespoon of olive oil and the parsley. Toss to mix and check the seasonings. Add salt and pepper if necessary. Serve hot or at room temperature.

Speedy Spiedini

Makes 4 to 6 servings

Spiedini, skewers or kabobs in Italian, are very quick to make once you've got the grill going. We use disposable wooden or bamboo skewers, which have to be soaked ahead of time. Spiedini are the perfect tidbits to serve guests who like to mill around the barbecue when you're grilling. We usually do some chicken and some shrimp to give everyone a choice.

4 tablespoons extra virgin olive oil

2 tablespoons fresh lemon juice

1 tablespoon chopped fresh parsley

¼ teaspoon kosher salt

Pinch freshly ground black pepper

¾-pound skinless chicken cutlet, cut into 12 long strips

1. Up to 1 day in advance, soak 12 wooden skewers in cold water to cover for 12 to 24 hours. Soaking will help keep the skewers from burning when the chicken is grilled.

2. Combine the olive oil, lemon juice, parsley, salt, and pepper in a bowl and beat until blended. Add the chicken and toss until coated with the marinade. Let stand at room temperature for 15 minutes to 1 hour.

3. Thread the chicken pieces onto the skewers, doubling back and forth a few times so the chicken is held securely on the skewer. Reserve any marinade in the bowl. *The chicken may be prepared to this point up to 2 hours in advance.*

4. Set up the grill, light the coals, and place the grill 4 inches above them. When the coals are ready, grill the chicken, turning often, until well browned and cooked through, about 4 minutes. Or lightly oil a broiler pan and heat it under the broiler until very hot; put the skewers on the pan and broil about 4 inches from the heat. Baste once or twice with the reserved marinade. Serve the skewers hot.

Sandwiches and Starters

Patti Shrimp

Makes 4 servings

This recipe comes to us from Patti Scialfa, who is as at home with a skillet in her hand as she is with a guitar. On its own it's a light but appetite-sparking first course. Spooned over linguine or spaghetti it's dinner.

1 pound medium (26 to 30 per pound) shrimp, peeled and deveined (see Note)

1 tablespoon Old Bay Seasoning

2 cloves garlic, minced

Freshly ground black pepper

2 tablespoons olive oil

¼ cup Chicken Broth, preferably homemade (page 53), or low-sodium canned broth

2 tablespoons unsalted butter

2 tablespoons lemon juice

2 tablespoons chopped fresh parsley (optional)

1. Toss the shrimp, Old Bay Seasoning, garlic, and pepper to taste in a bowl until the shrimp are coated with the seasoning. *The shrimp may be prepared to this point up to 1 day in advance. Refrigerate the shrimp, covered, until needed.*

2. Heat the olive oil in a large skillet over medium heat. Add the shrimp and toss just until they begin to turn pink, about 30 seconds. Add the broth, increase the heat to high and boil, shaking the pan occasionally, until the liquid is reduced by half, about 2 minutes. Add the butter, lemon juice, and parsley, if using, and boil until the butter is incorporated into the sauce and the shrimp are cooked through, about 1 minute. Serve hot.

Note: Peel off the shell of the shrimp a few sections at a time, leaving on the tail. Cut through the curved outer part of the shrimp and remove the vein that runs down the back. Rinse the shrimp under cold running water.

Grill the shrimp instead of sautéing them. Arrange the marinated, uncooked shrimp in a grill basket or thread them a few at a time on 2 parallel skewers (bamboo or wooden skewers have to be soaked in cold water first for at least 12 hours to prevent burning). Set up the grill, light the coals, and place the grill 4 inches above them. When the coals are ready, grill the shrimp, turning once, until they turn pink, about 3 minutes.

BCF Chicken Wings

Makes 4 servings

Chicken wings make the perfect handheld starter or snack, but too often they are greasy and unappetizing. Never ours. We slow-roast the wings first to render the fat, then grill them. You can make the wings hot with Blue Collar's 1-2-3 BBQ Sauce or sweet with our Teriyaki Sauce. Or make a batch of each and put the decision to vox populi.

2 pounds chicken wings, either whole or cut into sections
Kosher salt
Freshly ground black pepper
¼ cup Blue Collar's 1-2-3 BBQ Sauce (page 45) or Teriyaki Sauce
(page 44)

1. If you are using whole wings, cut off and discard the wing tips. Cut the remaining part of the wings in two at the joint.

2. Heat the oven to 350°F. Line a baking sheet with aluminum foil and set aside.

3. Place the wing pieces in a bowl, sprinkle them lightly with salt and pepper, and toss. Arrange the wings in a single layer on the baking sheet. Bake until the wings are golden brown and crisp, about 35 minutes. Remove to paper towels to drain. Transfer the wings to a bowl and toss with the sauce of your choice. *Wings may be prepared to this point up to 1 day in advance. Refrigerate, covered, until needed. Bring the wings to room temperature 30 minutes before cooking.*

4. Set up the grill, light the coals, and place the grill 4 inches above them. When the coals are ready, grill the wings about 4 inches from the coals until heated through and lightly browned, about 5 minutes. Or reheat them in a 350°F. oven until heated through, about 15 minutes. (Lining the baking sheet with aluminum foil again will save clean-up time.)

Baby Back Ribs

Makes 6 appetizer or 4 main-course servings

Our way of marinating and cooking ribs was inspired by Sylvia Woods of Sylvia's restaurant in Harlem. Of course Sylvia, being the Queen of Soul Food, would never use baby back ribs, but we like them now and then for a change.

3 pounds baby back ribs (about 2 slabs)

1 small red onion, thinly sliced

¾ cup apple juice or apple cider

1 teaspoon kosher salt

1 recipe Blue Collar's 1-2-3 BBQ Sauce (page 45) or Teriyaki Sauce (page 44)

1. Cut each slab of ribs into 2- to 3-bone sections. Toss the ribs in a large bowl with the onion, apple juice, and salt. Layer the ribs in a baking dish and pour the marinade over them. Refrigerate for at least 12 hours, turning once or twice.

2. Heat the oven to 350°F.

3. Cover the baking dish tightly with aluminum foil. Bake the ribs until they are very tender, about 1½ hours. Remove the cover and rotate the ribs half way through the baking. Cool the ribs to room temperature in the baking liquid.

4. Set up the grill, light the coals, and place the grill 4 inches above them. Coat the ribs with sauce. When the coals are ready, grill the ribs until well browned, turning as necessary so they brown evenly, about 5 minutes. Serve hot.

Teriyaki Sauce

Makes 1¼ cups

A little of our teriyaki goes a long way. Very lightly brush the food with it and let it stand at room temperature for about half an hour before grilling; baste occasionally with any sauce left in the dish. The food will brown very quickly, so cook thick pieces, like swordfish steak or pork chops, over slow coals. Serve teriyaki dishes with Coconut Rice (page 222) or Curried Rice (page 223) and Roasted Broccoli (page 196).

One 10-ounce bottle soy sauce, preferably low-sodium

¼ cup (packed) dark brown sugar

¼ cup rice wine, sake, or dry white wine

¼ cup rice wine vinegar or white wine vinegar

1 tablespoon finely chopped peeled fresh gingerroot

Combine all the ingredients in a small saucepan. Bring to a boil over medium heat and boil, uncovered, until reduced by half, about 10 minutes. *Sauce may be stored in a tightly covered jar in the refrigerator for up to 4 weeks.*

Like many of our recipes, this is a basic formula, one that has worked well for us. We are constantly altering it, adding fresh chiles, molasses, garlic, grilled onions instead of the white, or cider vinegar instead of lemon juice——depending on the occasion and the mood of the troops. This sauce is as easy as 1-2-3 to put together, so we know you'll soon be doing the same.

One 14-ounce bottle ketchup

½ cup warm water

1 small white onion, finely chopped

½ cup hot sauce, such as Red Devil, Crystal, or Tabasco

2 tablespoons fresh lemon juice

Combine all ingredients in a small heavy saucepan. Heat to simmering over medium heat. Remove from the heat and cool to room temperature. Puree in batches in a blender until smooth. *Sauce may be stored in a tightly covered jar in the refrigerator for up to 4 weeks.*

Soups

We make soup by the vat at Blue Collar Foods, both for catered events and for the retail establishments we supply also with sandwiches and desserts. It seems people really like honest soup, the kind we offer them.

The soups in this book are our best-sellers. With the exception of the Blue Collar Chicken Soup, which entails poaching a whole chicken, all of them can be made in a half hour or less if you have some homemade or canned broth on hand. Some don't even need broth. This means you can come home from work, shed your monkey suit, get the soup going, toss together a salad or sandwich, and eat forty-five minutes later——less time than it takes to have a meal in a cardboard box delivered. And it's a hell of a lot cheaper.

These are also good soups for parties. They are elegant enough to eat with a spoon at a sit-down dinner, casual enough to sip from a mug standing around at a barbecue or buffet dinner. Many can be served at room temperature, always a boon for entertaining.

Our chicken soup is how chicken soup ought to be—and used to be—with lots of poached chicken and vegetables floating in an honest homemade broth. We make it rather brothy, but you can add more vegetables, like string beans, bits of cauliflower, diced rutabaga, etc., if you prefer.

One 3½-pound chicken (see Note)

4 quarts cold water

4 to 5 carrots, peeled and diced (about 2 cups)

4 ribs celery, diced (about 2 cups)

2 medium onions, finely diced (about 2 cups)

½ pound mushrooms, thinly sliced (about 2 cups) (optional)

2 tablespoons chopped fresh parsley

Kosher salt

Freshly ground black pepper

1. Place the chicken in a 6- to 8-quart pot and pour in enough water to barely cover the chicken. Bring to a boil over high heat. Skim the foam and fat from the surface. Reduce the heat and simmer, uncovered, for 1 hour, turning the chicken over after 30 minutes. Continue to skim fat from the surface occasionally.

2. Remove the chicken to a platter or bowl to cool. (The best way to do this is to lift it by inserting a long-handled spoon into the cavity and letting the chicken drain over the pot for a second or two before gently moving the chicken to the platter.) Let the chicken stand until cool enough to handle. Add the carrots, celery, onions, and mushrooms, if using, to the broth and simmer for 30 minutes.

3. Strip the meat from the bones, discarding the fat and skin and shredding the meat into bite-size pieces as you go. Add the chicken meat and parsley to the broth. Stir in salt and pepper to taste. Simmer for 15 minutes. Check the seasoning and serve hot.

Note: An equal weight of chicken parts (legs, thighs, etc.) can be substituted for a whole chicken.

Variations

Chicken Rice Soup: Add 1½ cups cooked long-grain or brown rice to the finished soup. Cover and simmer for 5 minutes to warm through, stirring occasionally.

Cream of Chicken Soup: Dissolve 2 tablespoons cornstarch in ½ cup milk. Stir this mixture into the soup about 5 minutes before it is done. Simmer, stirring often, until the soup thickens.

Chicken Noodle Soup: Break enough long pasta (linguine, spaghetti, or angel hair, for example) into 2-inch lengths to measure 1 cup, more if you love a thick soup. Stir the pasta into the soup 5 minutes after adding the chicken meat in Step 3. Stir frequently until tender, 5 to 10 minutes.

Littlenecks in Broth

Makes 4 servings

This is the soup to have after "A pleasant walk, a pleasant talk / Along the briny beach," in the words of the Walrus. We think of it as best for the kind of impromptu summer occasion when someone shows up with a big sack full of really good clams, either from the shore or the store.

18 littleneck or other small hard-shell clams

6 scallions

2 cups Chicken Broth, preferably homemade (page 53), or low-sodium canned broth

2 slices lime

6 thin slices fresh gingerroot, peeled

1 tablespoon sherry

Large pinch crushed red pepper

1 tablespoon unsalted butter

1. Scrub the clams well under cold running water, removing as much sand as possible from the crevices. Drain well. Trim the scallions and slice them thin, keeping the green and white parts separate.

2. Combine the broth, lime slices, ginger, sherry, crushed red pepper, and white part of the scallions in a 3- to 4-quart saucepan. Bring to a boil over high heat. Reduce the heat and simmer, covered, for 10 minutes. Remove the lime and ginger slices with a slotted spoon. Add the clams and butter, increase the heat to high, and boil the clams, covered, until all are opened, about 5 minutes. Stir the clams once or twice. Discard any that don't open.

3. Divide the clams among 4 warmed serving bowls and ladle the broth over the clams. Sprinkle with scallion greens and serve at once.

White Bean and Lemon Soup

Makes 6 generous servings

Our white bean soup is infused with the subtle flavor of a whole lemon, a technique we borrowed from Middle Eastern cooking. If you have any soup left over, it will probably be thick enough by the next day to serve as a side dish, reheated in either a very low oven or a microwave oven.

2 tablespoons olive oil

1 rib celery, diced (about 1 cup)

1 small red onion, diced (about 1 cup)

1 medium carrot, peeled and diced (about 1 cup)

8 cups water or Chicken Broth (page 53)

1 lemon, quartered and seeds removed

½ teaspoon dried rosemary

¼ teaspoon freshly ground black pepper

1 pound navy beans, soaked (page 212)

2 tablespoons kosher salt

⅓ cup dried breadcrumbs, roasted (optional)

(continued)

1. Heat the olive oil in a 4- to 5-quart saucepan over medium heat. Add the celery, onion, and carrot and cook until the vegetables are soft, about 3 to 4 minutes. Add the water, lemon, rosemary, and pepper. Drain the beans and add them to the liquid. Heat to a boil, stirring occasionally. Reduce the heat, cover, and simmer for 30 to 40 minutes, or until the beans are very soft. Add the salt after 20 minutes.

2. Discard the pieces of lemon. Check the soup for seasoning. *The soup may be prepared up to 2 days in advance. Reheat over low heat. Thin with water if necessary and check the seasonings before serving.*

3. Serve hot, sprinkled with breadcrumbs, if desired.

Note: For a heartier soup, transfer about 1 cup of the soup to a blender in Step 2 and pulse until pureed. Stir the puree back into the soup.

Chicken Broth

Today's cook should never be without chicken broth, in the fridge, in the freezer, or in the can. It serves as the base for quick but flavorful soups and Skillet Meals (page 162), as well as sauces with a professional touch.

At Blue Collar Food, we make a lot of chicken broth. We take the bare bones of a poached chicken after stripping them of meat, as for Blue Collar Chicken Soup (page 48), or of a roast chicken after carving it, put them in a saucepan with water (about 2 quarts for the bones of 1 chicken), and simmer them for 2 to 3 hours, uncovered, over very low heat, to draw out every drop of flavor. Then we strain the broth, let it cool to room temperature, and refrigerate or freeze it until it's needed. The bones of 1 chicken will yield 5 to 6 cups of broth.

If you don't have a cooked chicken, make some broth with raw chicken necks and backs. A buck's worth (a little over a pound at today's prices) makes about 4 cups of broth. Just be sure to skim the foam that rises at the beginning and the fat at the end. Raw chicken bones require longer cooking, up to 6 hours.

You can also make an excellent broth from the bones and carcass of a roasted turkey, as described in Steps 1 and 2 of the recipe for Corn Chowder with Turkey (page 56).

Canned chicken broth, particularly the kind that is low in sodium, is a quite acceptable substitute for homemade broth.

Cabbage and Lamb Soup

Makes 6 servings

What is there about cabbage? You buy a head, make some coleslaw or boiled cabbage or whatever, and end up with half of it languishing in the vegetable drawer. What to do? We sometimes cut it up and fry it slowly in olive oil. Cooked like this, cabbage is utterly transformed—it's golden brown and sweet as sugar. You could toss in a few pitted black olives, too, just for the hell of it. Another discovery we're proud of is this hearty winter soup based on lamb shanks. For a couple of frugal guys like us, using such inexpensive cuts adds immeasurably to the appeal of soup making.

2 lamb shanks (about 2 pounds)

Kosher salt

Freshly ground black pepper

1 tablespoon vegetable oil

2 slices bacon or pancetta, if available, cut crosswise into ½-inch-wide
    pieces

2 medium carrots, cut into large dice (about 1½ cups)

3 ribs celery, cut into large dice (about 1½ cups)

1 medium onion, cut into large dice (about 1½ cups)

½ head green cabbage, cored and cut into large dice (about 5 cups)

1. Trim any excess fat from the shanks. Pat them dry with paper towels and sprinkle them with salt and pepper.

2. Heat the oil in a 4- to 5-quart pot over medium heat. Add the bacon and stir until browned, about 5 minutes. Remove with a slotted spoon to paper towels to drain. Place the shanks in the pot and brown slowly, turning as necessary, until golden on all sides, about 10 minutes. Drain the shanks on paper towels and pour off the oil from the pan. Return the shanks to the pot and pour in enough water to cover the shanks. Bring to a boil over high heat, reduce the heat, cover the pot, and simmer for 45 minutes, turning the shanks once after 20 minutes.

   3.   Add the carrots, celery, onion, cabbage, 1 tablespoon salt, and ¼ teaspoon pepper. Cook until the lamb shanks are tender, about 30 minutes. Remove the shanks to a plate and let them stand until cool enough to handle.

   4.   Remove the meat from the bones and coarsely shred it, removing any gristle. Return the meat to the pot, heat to simmering, and check the seasoning. Serve hot.

   Note: You may substitute a meaty bone left from a roasted leg of lamb for the lamb shanks called for in the recipe.

The soup pot: last stop for the Thanksgiving bird. The bones and carcass make a strong broth, overpowering perhaps for a delicate soup but perfect for one like this that is full of its own rich flavors. You'll have to use frozen corn in November; fortunately it's a vegetable that freezes well.

Meaty bones from a roasted turkey, carcass broken if necessary to fit in
    pot (see Note)

4 quarts cold water

3 tablespoons unsalted butter

2 medium carrots, cut into medium dice (about 1½ cups)

2 ribs celery, cut into medium dice (about 1½ cups)

1 medium onion, cut into medium dice (about 1½ cups)

2 ears fresh corn, kernels removed, or 2 cups frozen corn kernels

3 tablespoons all-purpose flour

4 medium red potatoes, cut into medium dice (about 1½ cups)

Kosher salt

Freshly ground black pepper

1 cup cream, milk, or half-and-half

Chopped fresh parsley or cilantro (optional)

1. Place the bones in a 6- to 8-quart pot and pour in enough water to barely cover them. Bring to a boil over high heat. Skim the foam and fat from the surface. Reduce the heat and simmer, uncovered, for 1 hour. Continue to skim fat from the surface occasionally.

2.   Remove the bones to a platter or bowl to cool, using tongs if the bones are breaking apart. Let stand until cool enough to handle. Remove any meat from the bones and cut into ¼-inch dice. Reserve 2 cups of the meat, return the bones to the broth, and simmer for 1 hour. Strain the broth. Reserve 4 cups for this recipe and keep it hot. Save the remaining broth for another use. Save any extra meat in the freezer for soups or low-fat meat sauces for pasta.

3.   Heat the butter in 4- to 5-quart pot over low heat. Add the carrots, celery, onion, and corn and sauté until softened, about 2 to 3 minutes. Add the flour and cook until the mixture begins to stick to the bottom of the pot. Slowly ladle the hot broth into the pot, stirring constantly to prevent sticking. Stir until the soup is thickened and simmering. Let the soup simmer for 5 minutes.

4.   Add the turkey meat and potatoes. Increase the heat to high and bring the soup to a boil. Reduce heat to a simmer, add salt and pepper to taste, and simmer for 15 minutes, stirring occasionally to prevent sticking. *The soup may be prepared to this point up to 2 days in advance.*

Reheat over low heat. Stir in the cream, check the seasonings, and simmer for 5 minutes longer. Sprinkle with parsley, if desired. Serve hot.

Notes: Substitute 4 pounds turkey drumsticks and/or wings. This broth will not be as rich as that made from roasted-turkey bones.

If turkey is not available, substitute 4 cups canned or homemade Chicken Broth (page 53) in Step 3.

Roasted Eggplant Soup

Makes 6 servings

It's very difficult to identify the main ingredient in this richly flavored, unusual soup since eggplant when roasted takes on a smoky, mysterious flavor. Our editor, Harriet Bell, served this to her 10-year-old son and his friends, and they didn't even say "yuck." At least not until they found out what it was.

2 large eggplants (about 1¾ pounds)

Olive oil

6 scallions

1½ cups water

One 11½-ounce can V-8™ vegetable juice (see Note)

½ cup Italian (flat-leaf) parsley leaves

3 cloves garlic, peeled

2 teaspoons kosher salt

Freshly ground black pepper

Plain yogurt (optional)

1. Preheat the oven to 350°F.

2. Cut the eggplant in half lengthwise and brush the cut sides lightly with olive oil. Roast the eggplants, cut side down, on a baking sheet until very tender and well browned, about 30 minutes. Let the eggplant cool completely.

3. Scoop out as much pulp as possible and place in a 4- to 5-quart pot. Add the remaining ingredients, except the yogurt, and bring to a boil. Reduce the heat, cover the pot, and simmer for 15 minutes. Cool the soup slightly.

4.   Puree in batches in a blender, scraping down the sides as needed. Pulse the blender on and off for a chunky puree or leave it running until the soup is very smooth, as you wish. *The soup may be prepared up to 2 days in advance. Reheat over low heat and check the seasonings before serving.*

5.   Serve hot, with a dollop of yogurt if desired.

Note: Substitute ¾ cup tomato juice and ¾ cup water for the vegetable juice.

Finocchio Soup

Makes 4 servings

Finocchio—not to be confused with Pinocchio—is a vegetable of Mediterranean origins that has become almost commonplace in larger supermarkets and food specialty stores over the past decade. Known in English as fennel, it is in season in fall and winter. It makes a hearty soup, especially if you include some chicken. This is good to serve in mugs at a buffet supper.

1 medium bulb fresh fennel (about 1¼ pounds)

2 tablespoons olive oil

1 chicken leg, raw or cooked

1 large onion, peeled and thinly sliced

2 cloves garlic, thinly sliced (optional)

3 cups Chicken Broth, preferably homemade (page 53), or low-sodium canned broth

1 medium russet potato, peeled and cut into ½-inch pieces

1 tablespoon lemon juice

Kosher salt

Freshly ground black pepper

1. Trim the fennel, removing the stalks if still attached. Coarsely chop some of the fine fronds. Reserve about 3 tablespoons. Cut the fennel bulb in half and cut out the core. Thinly slice the fennel.

2. Heat the oil in a 2- to 3-quart pot over medium heat. Add the chicken leg, onion, garlic, and sliced fennel. Reduce the heat to low, cover, and simmer, stirring once or twice, until the vegetables are tender, about 15 minutes. Remove the cover, increase the heat to medium, and cook, stirring occasionally, until the vegetables are lightly browned, about 5 minutes.

3.   Add the broth and potato to the pot. Bring to a boil, reduce the heat, and simmer, covered, until the potato is tender, about 10 minutes. (If you started with a raw chicken leg check to make sure it is fully cooked. Cook a little longer if necessary.)

4.   With a slotted spoon, remove the chicken leg and about 1 cup of the vegetables to a plate. Pick out any garlic cloves and return them to the pot. Let the soup cool slightly. Puree the soup, either in a blender or by passing it through a food mill. Pick the chicken meat from the bones, coarsely shred it, and return it and the vegetables to the pot. Heat to simmering, and stir in the lemon juice and salt and pepper to taste. Serve hot, sprinkled with some of the reserved fennel leaves. *The soup may be prepared up to 2 days in advance. Reheat over low heat and check the seasonings before serving.*

Basic Soup Making Tips

How to Make a Cream-of Soup

Most cream-of soups start out as a vegetable puree. Whether to add cream—or sour cream or milk or buttermilk—or any other ingredient is the cook's choice. Sometimes, as in our Creamless of Tomato Soup, there is no dairy product at all. Instead, rice is cooked in with the vegetables to give the soup a creamy texture.

To make this kind of soup, begin by cooking a member of the onion family—white or red onions, leeks, scallions, and/or garlic—in a little butter or oil. When tender, add the other vegetable—mushrooms or fennel or tomatoes—and sauté until the pieces soften. Add enough liquid—broth or water—to barely cover the ingredients and bring the whole thing to a boil. Reduce the heat, cover the pot, and simmer until the vegetables are very tender. During this simmering period, you can add a compatible herb or spice seasoning—basil with tomatoes, parsley with eggplant, for example—if you like.

Once the vegetables are tender, set some aside and puree the rest. You can do this in batches in a blender or food processor, turning the machine quickly on and off and scraping down the sides as necessary. The puree can be chunky or smooth, however you like it. You can also pass the soup through a hand-operated food mill, which will make a fine or coarse puree depending on which blade you use.

Just before serving, reheat the puree, add the milk product you want, and check the seasoning. Add the vegetables you've set aside and/or pieces of meat if you have some and heat through. Sprinkle with chopped herbs—parsley, basil, cilantro, chives—and serve. Cold soups can be completed before or after refrigerating them. Be sure to taste and adjust the seasoning before serving: Chilling mutes a lot of flavors, especially salt.

How to Make Vegetable Soup

Vegetable soups start out with a base of aromatic root vegetables—onions or leeks, carrots, turnips, parsnips—and sometimes celery. "Sweat" pieces of these vegetables in butter or oil, that is, sauté them slowly, covered, until they give off juice.

Add liquid—broth, water mixed with tomato juice, vegetable cooking liquid, just plain water—bring to a boil, add some other vegetables, and simmer until they are tender. These other vegetables might include string beans, peas, cauliflower, broccoli, or zucchini, for example. Season the soup to taste with salt and pepper, chopped fresh herbs, dried spices like nutmeg or paprika, lemon juice, or whatever else imagination and experience lead you to.

How to Make Soup with Leftover Meat and Poultry

Having leftover poultry or meat is almost as good as having some homemade broth. Start the vegetables as you would for a vegetable soup. Add the leftover meat, preferably on the bone, when you add the liquid. Wait to add the second group of vegetables. Simmer until the meat is very tender. Remove it from the pot to cool, strip it from the bone if necessary, and cut it into small chunks. Put the meat back in the soup when you add the second group of vegetables. As always, check the seasoning before serving.

How to Cool and Store Soups

Whether you plan to refrigerate or freeze your soup, it is best to cool it to room temperature first. In a restaurant kitchen this is done by transferring the soup to a storage container, packing it in a sinkful of ice, and stirring it occasionally until it is lightly chilled. You can approximate this at home by placing the soup in its storage container in the sink and running enough cold water to come two thirds of the way up the container. Be careful not to get any in the soup. Stir occasionally until the soup is cool. Replace the water in the sink with more cold water if necessary. Cover the container and store in the refrigerator or freezer.

Mushroom-Buttermilk Soup

Makes 4 servings

We use a quarter of a pound of mixed button mushrooms and fresh shiitakes per portion of this densely rich soup, which can be served hot or chilled. Buttermilk adds the richness of cream but only a fraction of the fat and calories. If you can't find shiitakes, substitute cremini or a handful of wild mushrooms or make the soup with button mushrooms alone.

One pound of mushrooms may seem like a lot for four servings, but they cook down to a very small amount, making a richly flavored soup.

¾ pound button mushrooms, wiped clean

¼ pound fresh shiitake mushrooms, wiped clean

2 tablespoons unsalted butter or margarine

2 tablespoons olive oil

1 medium onion, thinly sliced

2 inner ribs celery, with leaves, sliced

1 clove garlic, crushed

1 tablespoon all-purpose flour

4 cups hot Chicken Broth, preferably homemade (page 53), or low-sodium canned broth

1½ cups buttermilk

¼ cup chopped fresh parsley

2 teaspoons kosher salt

½ teaspoon freshly ground black pepper

Croutons (page 81)

1. Remove the stems from both types of mushrooms. Trim off any hard or soft parts and set the stems aside. Slice the caps about ¼ inch thick and set them aside separately.

2.   Heat the butter and oil in a 4-quart saucepan over medium heat until the butter is foaming. Add the onion, celery, garlic, and mushroom stems. Sauté, stirring occasionally, until the onions are tender and lightly browned, about 10 minutes. Adjust the heat so the vegetables don't burn before they are tender.

3.   Add the flour and stir until it coats the vegetables and is lightly browned, about 4 minutes. Add the broth slowly, stirring constantly, making sure to scrape the bottom. The liquid should thicken gradually. Bring the soup to a boil, stirring constantly, reduce the heat, and simmer until the vegetables are very tender, about 10 minutes.

4.   Remove the vegetables with a slotted spoon to a blender. Blend until smooth, adding a little of the liquid if necessary. Return the puree to the pan and add the buttermilk, parsley, salt, pepper, and sliced mushroom caps. Simmer until the mushrooms are tender, about 10 minutes. *The soup may be prepared entirely in advance and refrigerated for up to 3 days.*

5.   To serve the soup, reheat if necessary, check the seasonings, and ladle into bowls or mugs. Put 3 or 4 croutons on top and pass the rest.

Note: The best way to clean mushrooms is to wipe them with either the palm of your hand or a paper towel. Mushrooms absorb water like a sponge, so you should avoid washing them before cooking.

Red Potato Vichyssoise

Makes 6 servings

With this soup you save time—by scrubbing the potatoes instead of peeling them; lose fat—by thinning with milk instead of cream; and gain flavor—by using scallions instead of leeks. This is one of our most popular soups, whether served hot or cold.

1 pound small red potatoes, scrubbed

12 scallions

2 tablespoons unsalted butter

3 cups Chicken Broth (page 53) or water

1 teaspoon kosher salt

½ teaspoon freshly ground black pepper

3 cups cold skim or whole milk

1. Cut the potatoes into small pieces, dropping them into cold water to cover if the soup is not going to be made right away. Trim the scallions. Coarsely chop the white part and finely chop some of the green. Set aside separately.

2. Melt the butter in a saucepan over medium heat, add the white part of the scallions and cook until soft. Drain potatoes if necessary and add to scallions. Add the broth, salt, and pepper. Cook, uncovered, over medium heat until the potatoes are soft, about 30 minutes. Remove from the heat and let cool.

3. Puree the soup in batches in a blender or pass it through a food mill fitted with the finest blade. *Soup may be prepared to this point up to 1 day in advance and refrigerated.*

4. When ready to serve, add the milk and stir well. Check the seasonings and adjust if necessary. Serve the soup cold or reheat it over low heat. Either way, sprinkle each serving with some of the reserved scallion greens.

Creamless of Tomato Soup

Makes 6 servings

Made with canned Italian-style tomatoes in the dead of winter, this soup says "Thanks for the memory." Serve it hot in bowls or mugs. In summer, make the soup with vine-ripened tomatoes, thin it with a little cream, and serve it hot or cold. You'll find a little rice cooked with the vegetables goes a remarkably long way toward thickening a pureed soup like this one and giving it a silky texture.

1 tablespoon olive oil

1 medium red onion, finely chopped

2 small cloves garlic, finely chopped

2 tablespoons long-grain rice

Two 28-ounce cans Italian-style plum tomatoes, with their liquid, or 4 pounds fresh plum tomatoes, peeled and seeded (see page 68)

2 cups Chicken Broth (page 53) or water

2 tablespoons chopped fresh parsley or basil

Grated parmesan (optional)

1. Heat the oil in a 4- to 5-quart pot over medium heat. Add the onion and garlic and sauté until softened, about 2 minutes. Add the rice and cook, stirring, 1 to 2 minutes more. Stir in the tomatoes and broth. Heat the mixture to a boil, reduce the heat, and simmer, covered, stirring occasionally, until the rice is very tender, about 20 minutes. Remove the soup from the heat and let stand until slightly cooled. Puree the soup in batches in a blender until smooth. *Soup may be prepared to this point up to 1 day in advance and refrigerated.*

2. When ready to serve, reheat the soup over low heat, stirring constantly so that it does not burn on the bottom. Adjust the seasoning if necessary and ladle into warm soup bowls or mugs. Garnish with parsley or basil and grated parmesan, if desired. To serve cold, remove the soup from the fridge, adjust the seasoning, and ladle into cold bowls or mugs. Garnish with parsley or basil.

Soups

How to Peel and Seed Tomatoes

Bring a large pot of water to a boil. Cut the cores out of the tomatoes and cut a small "x" in the opposite end. Add the tomatoes to the boiling water and blanch them until the skins loosen, 1 to 2 minutes, depending on the tomatoes. Keep the tomatoes in the water just long enough to loosen the skins; overblanching can make them soggy. Remove the tomatoes to a colander with a slotted spoon and run them under cold water until cool. If necessary, let the water return to a boil and repeat with any remaining tomatoes. Slip the skins off the blanched tomatoes. Cut the tomatoes in half, lengthwise for plum tomatoes, crosswise for round tomatoes. Flick out the seeds with your fingers.

Zucchini and Tomato Soup

Makes 6 servings

Like many of our soups, this one takes only thirty minutes from start to finish, enough time to put together a sandwich or salad to round out the meal. It's a chunky soup, as good—maybe even better—at room temperature as it is hot.

2 pounds fresh tomatoes, peeled and seeded (page 68)

1 pound zucchini

2 tablespoons olive oil

1 small white onion, peeled, cut in half, and thinly sliced

2 cups Chicken Broth, preferably homemade (page 53), or low-sodium canned broth

1 teaspoon kosher salt

¼ teaspoon freshly ground black pepper

¼ cup chopped fresh basil or parsley

1. Chop the tomatoes. Scrub the zucchini, cut in half lengthwise, then crosswise into ¼-inch slices.

2. Heat the oil in a 3- to 4-quart saucepan over medium heat. Add the onion and cook until softened, about 2 minutes. Add the tomato. Cook over medium heat, stirring constantly, until the tomato begins to soften, about 4 minutes. Reduce the heat to low, add the zucchini, broth, salt, and pepper and cover the pan. Cook for about 20 minutes, or until the zucchini is very tender. Add the basil after 10 minutes. Taste and adjust the seasoning if necessary before serving. Serve hot or at room temperature.

Note: If tomatoes are not dead ripe, substitute one 28-ounce can Italian-style plum tomatoes, with their liquid, for the fresh tomatoes. Roughly chop the canned tomatoes before adding them in Step 2.

This minestrone is chockablock with vegetables, more like a ratatouille than a conventional soup. Think of the recipe as a blueprint, and substitute, add, or omit vegetables as you will, depending on availability. Layering the vegetables is what counts; it allows them to cook without burning. Always start with the vegetable highest in water content, like tomato, at the bottom. Serve the minestrone at room temperature with some freshly shaved parmesan for a real summer treat. It's also a good soup to have hot or spooned over rice for a meal-in-one.

1 head romaine lettuce

4 large ripe tomatoes, cored and cut into ¼-inch slices

4 small zucchini, scrubbed and cut into ¼-inch rounds (about 3 cups)

4 small yellow squash, scrubbed and cut into ¼-inch rounds (about 3 cups)

1 cup fresh or frozen peas

1 small red onion, cut into ¼-inch slices and separated into rings (about 1 cup)

¼ cup extra virgin olive oil

Kosher salt

Freshly ground black pepper

¼ pound piece parmesan, shaved

1.   Remove the dark outer leaves from the romaine. Cut the head into quarters lengthwise, then cut crosswise into ¼-inch strips. Wash and drain the lettuce. Line up the lettuce and all the other vegetables side by side on the work surface and visually divide them into 4 equal portions.

2. Coat the bottom of a heavy 4- to 5-quart pot with a tight-fitting lid with a little of the olive oil. Begin layering the vegetables in the pot, starting with a fourth each of the tomatoes, zucchini, yellow squash, romaine, peas, and onion. Sprinkle the top lightly with salt and pepper and some of the remaining olive oil. Make 3 more layers using the remaining vegetables, salt, pepper, and olive oil. (The vegetables will shrink with cooking, so be careful not to overseason.)

3. Cover the pot tightly and cook over high heat for 10 minutes without opening. Stir well and reduce the heat to medium. Cover and cook until the vegetables are very tender, about 10 minutes. Check the seasoning and serve immediately or let cool to room temperature and serve with parmesan shavings.

Pack this summer nectar in a thermos for picnics and barbecues and pour it into glass mugs or goblets on arrival. No spoons needed. The basil and jalapeño are not traditional, but nobody we know seems to mind.

4 ripe medium tomatoes, cored and cut into 2-inch chunks
(about 1½ pounds)

2 cucumbers, peeled, seeded, and cut into 1-inch chunks

2 yellow or red bell peppers, cored, seeded, and cut into 2-inch chunks

1 small red onion, thinly sliced

¼ cup olive oil, preferably extra virgin

¼ cup coarsely chopped fresh basil

2 tablespoons red wine vinegar

2 cloves garlic, minced

1 jalapeño, cored, seeded, and minced

2 teaspoons kosher salt

Combine all the ingredients in a large bowl and toss to mix. Transfer about a fourth of the mixture (including some of the liquid) to a food processor. Pulse until the mixture is finely chopped but not pureed. Repeat with the remaining vegetable mixture. *Soup may be made in advance and refrigerated for up to 3 days.* Remove from the refrigerator and let stand at room temperature for 20 minutes before serving.

Note: The soup can be prepared in a blender: Pulse the vegetable mixture in smaller batches stopping once or twice each time to scrape down the sides.

Salads

Blue Collar Food's way of menu planning is to feature a lot of little tastes. We decide on one or two main courses, then choose small dishes to surround them. Salads have been our salvation. We always put a big mixed salad on the menu, like the BCF Caesar Salad or the Tricolor Salad with Gruyère, and often one or more of the other vegetable salads in this chapter.

In building our salad repertoire, we dug deep into our culinary baggage. We needed to find salads that could stand up to unpredictable conditions and never look tired or wilted. So we developed a couple of basic salad dressings that won't cook the greens while they sit out. We found combinations of sturdy greens that can take a lot of abuse en route. And we kept our options open with salads that don't call for greens at all and/or don't have to be served chilled.

What's amazing is that these salads, which we created for our business, are so well suited to smaller-scale home entertaining. Best of all, many of them answer the cry of "Help! I just got home, I'm hungry, and I'm too tired to cook." With greens and some fresh herbs in the crisper, cheese in the fridge, and a tomato on the windowsill (or canned beets in the cupboard), you can throw together almost any of these salads in no time flat. Add some leftover chicken or canned tuna, and you've got it made.

House Ranch Dressing

Makes 3 cups

Used in minute quantities, as they are here, garlic and onion powder lend a little kick to dressings. Don't use too much, however, or you will find yourself with a dressing with that commercial salad bar taste.

¾ cup buttermilk

¾ cup mayonnaise

¾ cup sour cream

1 tablespoon dried chives or chopped fresh parsley (optional)

1 tablespoon white vinegar

1 teaspoon kosher salt

½ teaspoon onion powder

¼ teaspoon garlic powder

¼ teaspoon freshly ground black pepper

Combine all the ingredients in a bowl and whisk until thoroughly blended. Pour into a lidded container and refrigerate until ready to use. *The dressing may be stored in the coldest part of the refrigerator for up to 1 week. Shake vigorously before serving.*

While particularly apt for BCF Tricolor Salad, this dressing is suitable for any green salad made with sturdy greens. It's also good spooned over grilled chicken or salmon.

½ cup lightly toasted walnuts (see Note)

¼ cup raspberry vinegar or mild red wine vinegar

1 tablespoon honey

½ cup olive oil

½ cup vegetable oil

Kosher salt

Freshly ground black pepper

Combine the walnuts, vinegar, and honey in a blender. Blend on low speed until smooth. Combine the oils. With the motor running, add the oil very slowly in a thin stream. Continue until all the oil is incorporated. Season to taste with salt and pepper. *The dressing may be made up to 2 days in advance. Bring to room temperature at least 30 minutes before serving and check the seasoning.*

Note: Toast the walnuts in a small skillet over medium-low heat, stirring frequently, until they begin to brown, about 5 minutes. Remove from the pan immediately and let cool. If you are making this for the Tricolor Salad, toast 1 cup of walnuts and divide them evenly between the 2 recipes.

How to Make a Green Salad

The best green salads are made from lettuce that was just picked in the garden, quickly rinsed and lightly chilled, then tossed with a dressing made for the occasion from the best olive oil and mellow vinegar or mild lemon juice. Alas! The pleasure is denied to most of us, and even those who have gardens can usually grow lettuce only in the spring and fall.

Commercial lettuce growers and importers have come to the rescue. After years of limiting their customers to iceberg, romaine, and the occasional head of Boston, they started a few years ago to offer a dizzying choice of greens—the aforementioned staples as well as green or red loose leaf lettuce and oak leaf, red romaine, and Bibb and other butterheads. Such exotic greens as Belgian endive, mâche or corn salad, frisée (tender curly endive), radicchio, lolla rossa, and mizuna, are often available in specialty markets, as is the mix of tender seedling greens and herbs called mesclun. In addition, the more bitter greens, like watercress, escarole, arugula, and spinach, are sold virtually year round.

Buying salad greens. At Blue Collar Food, we always include a big green salad when we plan a meal. Our modus operandi is to look over what's on the market and pick by looks and price, with one or two luxury items thrown in. When we cater, we want salads that don't need pampering, so we tend to buy a mix of sturdier greens, say romaine, radicchio, and frisée. We also try to match mild and bitter greens that complement each other, like the classic combination of Belgian endive and watercress or butterhead and mâche. You can follow our m.o. in the supermarket; only the price will differ.

Washing and storing salad greens. If you are going to use the greens within the next two days, wash them right away and spin them absolutely dry. We recommend using a salad spinner. Now that many markets spray the produce to make it look fresh, it's particularly important to get your greens clean and dry as soon as possible. Store the greens in plastic bags in the vegetable drawer of the refrigerator.

Dressing the salad. We propose two all-purpose salad dressings in this chapter: a mellow vinaigrette and a creamy ranch dressing. The vinaigrette is good with green salads and potato salad, the ranch with green salads, vegetable slaw, and crudités. Both of these can be made in quantity and refrigerated for up to 1 week. In addition, we offer our special nut dressing, which was designed for the tricolor salad but can be used with any green salad; it does not keep as well as the others.

Tossing the salad. When you are ready to make the salad, tear the greens and place them in a large bowl, allowing about 1½ cups of greens per serving. Sprinkle lightly with kosher salt and freshly ground black pepper, if desired. Toss while dry to distribute the greens evenly. Add just enough dressing (about 2 tablespoons per serving) to lightly coat the greens and toss well. Serve immediately.

Lavishing the salad. If you want to add to your green salad, consider chopped scallions or red onion, grated carrot, sliced or diced cucumber, tomato wedges, and/or croutons. For an even more substantial salad, add some crumbled blue cheese or feta, or drained canned tuna, or leftover chicken, etc.

We used to work with a guy named Jeff Kent. At the end of the day, he would take a large bowl, head for the walk-in, and fill the bowl with a variety of greens and whatever stood in his path—the last piece of rabbit from the day's specials, some sliced beets in olive oil, a handful of walnuts. Home cooks don't have his options, but they do usually have more than they think in the fridge and cupboard. The sky's the limit here.

House Vinaigrette
Makes 1½ cups

Both of us were trained in the classical European tradition, and how to balance oils and vinegars for vinaigrette was drilled into us early on. Of course, no two masters agreed, but when we got together, we had to. The formula we finally settled on for Blue Collar salads is somewhat unconventional. We use two kinds of vinegar and two kinds of oil, and we upped the ante to six parts oil to one part vinegar, as opposed to the usual three or four to one. We find that this ratio makes for a smooth and mellow dressing with no acrid aftertaste.

3 tablespoons sherry vinegar or cider vinegar (see Note)
1 tablespoon balsamic vinegar
2 tablespoons Dijon mustard
1 teaspoon dried tarragon
½ teaspoon kosher salt
¼ teaspoon freshly ground black pepper
1 cup olive oil
½ cup walnut oil or peanut oil

1. Combine the vinegars, mustard, tarragon, salt, and pepper in a bowl and whisk until thoroughly blended. (Placing a damp towel under the bowl will help keep it steady while you whisk.) Pour in the oil very slowly, whisking, until all of it is incorporated. The dressing should look emulsified. Use immediately or store in the refrigerator in a jar with a tight-fitting lid. *The vinaigrette may be refrigerated for up to 1 week.*

2. Bring the dressing to room temperature, shake vigorously, and check the seasonings before serving. Use about 2 tablespoons per serving of salad.

Note: Taste your cider vinegar. Much of what is commonly available is too harsh for salad dressing. If that is the case, mellow the vinegar with the addition of a little apple juice or cider.

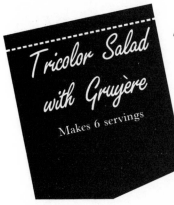

Tricolor Salad
with Gruyère

Makes 6 servings

It's easy for people who work with food all the time to make false assumptions about the way people eat. Doesn't everyone like liver? Isn't the whole world mad for dried tuna roe? Wouldn't anyone prefer a salad made of bitter greens to the same old thing? Well, maybe; then again, maybe not. Yet this salad is one of the most popular on our catering menu.

½ pound or half 10-ounce cellophane pack spinach, stemmed and cut
   into ½-inch strips

1 large head Belgian endive, cut in half lengthwise, cored, and cut
   crosswise into ½-inch strips

1 small head radicchio, cut in half, cored, and cut into ½-inch strips

1 cup coarsely grated gruyère (about 3 ounces)

½ cup lightly toasted chopped walnuts (page 75)

½ cup Toasted Walnut Dressing (page 75)

Kosher salt

Freshly ground black pepper

Combine the greens, gruyère, walnuts, and dressing in a large bowl. Toss well and check for seasoning. Serve immediately.

BCF Caesar Salad

Makes 6 servings

Our Caesar salad, either plain or topped with a grilled chicken breast, tops the charts at BCF. The salad is tossed with a light lemony dressing with only a touch of anchovy—which you could eliminate altogether if you don't like it or don't have it on hand. We poach the egg yolk in lemon juice for safety's sake, rather than eliminate this traditional touch. If you're looking to save time, use storebought croutons, the plain kind.

¼ cup fresh lemon juice

1 egg yolk

4 anchovy fillets or 2 teaspoons anchovy paste, or to taste

1 large clove garlic, chopped

1 teaspoon Dijon mustard

½ teaspoon Worcestershire sauce

1 cup olive oil

¼ cup grated parmesan

½ teaspoon cracked black pepper

Kosher salt

Piece of parmesan, for shaving

1 large head romaine lettuce

2 cups croutons (see Note)

1. Combine the lemon juice and egg yolk in a very small saucepan. Heat over medium heat until the egg yolk is cooked through, about 2 minutes. Transfer the juice and yolk to a blender jar and add the anchovies, garlic, mustard, and Worcestershire sauce. Blend until smooth. With the motor running, slowly add all but 2 tablespoons of the olive oil. Continue blending until all the oil is incorporated. (If the dressing becomes too thick and the oil begins to float on the surface add 1 tablespoon hot water.) Pour the dressing into a bowl, using a rubber spatula to get as much as possible out of the blender. Stir in the grated parmesan and black pepper. Taste and add salt if necessary.

2. Using a vegetable peeler, shave the block of parmesan into large curls. (This is easier to do if the parmesan is at room temperature.) You'll need about 10 curls for each serving. Refrigerate the curls in a covered container as soon as they're made.

3. Remove the outer leaves from the romaine. Tear the remaining leaves into large bite-size pieces, removing the very thick part of the rib of each leaf as you go. Wash the lettuce well and drain it thoroughly, preferably in a salad spinner. *Recipe may be prepared to this point up to 1 day in advance and the dressing, parmesan curls, and romaine refrigerated.*

4. When ready to serve, combine the lettuce, croutons, and dressing in a large bowl. Toss until the leaves are coated with dressing. Divide among serving plates and top each salad with some of the parmesan curls. Serve at once. Pass a pepper mill separately if you like.

Note: To make your own croutons, preheat the oven to 350°F. Cut 3 slices of day-old white bread into ½-inch cubes; you should have about 2 cups. Coat the sides of a mixing bowl with 2 tablespoons olive oil, add the bread cubes, and toss to coat. Turn the cubes onto a baking sheet and bake, stirring once or twice, until golden brown, about 12 minutes.

Bread, Tomato, and Basil Salad

Makes 4 servings

The Italian name for this salad is _panzanella_, or little swamp in Tuscan dialect. That should give you an idea of the right consistency. We usually make it with a rustic Italian bread, but it also works with whole wheat or sourdough bread (hear those Tuscans howl!). You can also substitute fresh rosemary for the basil if you are serving it with lamb.

3 tablespoons extra virgin olive oil
2 tablespoons red wine vinegar
2 tablespoons finely chopped red onion
Pinch freshly ground black pepper
1 ripe large tomato, cored and cut into ½-inch cubes
2 cups ½-inch cubes day-old Italian bread
¼ cup chopped fresh basil
Kosher salt, if necessary

1. Combine the olive oil, vinegar, and onion in a large bowl and let stand at room temperature for at least 15 minutes or up to 1 hour.

2. About 5 to 10 minutes before serving, add the pepper, tomato, bread, and basil to the bowl and toss until the bread has absorbed the liquid and the onion and basil are evenly distributed. Check the seasoning, add salt if necessary, and let stand a few minutes before serving.

Tomato-Feta Salad with Fresh Dill

Makes 2 servings

This salad is a spin-off of tomato-mozzarella-basil salad, by now almost a culinary cliché. The longer the salad stands, the better it is. If you like, you can serve it on a bed of mixed greens, like watercress and/or romaine or toss the greens into the salad.

2 ripe large tomatoes, cored and cut into eighths (about 1 pound)

½ cup crumbled feta cheese (2 ounces)

¼ cup olive oil

1 tablespoon balsamic vinegar

1 teaspoon chopped fresh dill

½ teaspoon kosher salt

Freshly ground black pepper

Place all the ingredients in a bowl and toss until the tomatoes are coated with dressing and the feta and dill are evenly distributed. Let stand for up to 1 hour before serving or refrigerate for up to 4 hours.

Note: Sheep's milk feta cheese preserved in brine is imported from several countries. It can be very strong and salty. If possible, taste the different kinds and pick the mildest, creamiest one. If your only choice is the bottled feta sold in supermarkets, rinse the cheese under cold running water. Put the feta in a container with a lid, cover with cold water, and store in the refrigerator until ready to use. Change the water every day.

Warm Beet and Goat Cheese Salad

Makes 4 servings

We feel sorry for the beet. It has everything going for it — good looks, great flavor, low cost — and still it's ignored. It must be the stains, but for those we blame not the beet but the eater. For this salad, we recommend roasting fresh beets; you can use canned beets instead if you're pressed for time. For a main course for two, divide the salad in half and top each portion with a grilled chicken breast or thin slices of London broil.

4 to 5 medium beets, with greens if possible (about 1¾ pounds)

2 tablespoons extra virgin olive oil

1 tablespoon sherry vinegar, or mellow red wine vinegar

¼ teaspoon kosher salt

Freshly ground black pepper

½ cup crumbled goat cheese (2 ounces)

1 small bunch flat-leaf spinach, stemmed, washed, and rinsed (about 8 ounces)

1.   Heat the oven to 375°F.

2.   Cut the beet stems to about 1 inch from the root. (You may use the thin, fresh-looking beet greens to replace some of the spinach called for in the recipe.) Poke each beet through the skin with a fork twice. Roast the beets directly on the oven rack until they are tender, 45 minutes to 1 hour. Let them cool to lukewarm. Slip off the skins. It may be necessary to cut away part of the skin. The beets will temporarily stain your hands purple, so you may want to wear gloves. Slice the beets about ½ inch thick.

3. Turn down the oven to 350°F. Place the beets in a bowl. Add the olive oil, vinegar, salt, and pepper. Toss until the beets are coated. Arrange the beets in a single layer in a baking dish and sprinkle the goat cheese on top. Bake until the cheese is softened and the beets are warmed through, about 5 minutes.

4. Return the beets to the bowl, add the spinach, and toss until the ingredients are evenly mixed. Serve at once.

Note: One 16-ounce can of sliced beets may be substituted for the fresh beets. Drain the beets well.

Watercress and Orange Salad with Roquefort

Makes 4 servings

Strong flavors and bright colors are a Blue Collar thing, and this salad certainly meets our criteria. Serve it with Grilled Chicken Breasts (page 134) or Grilled Butterflied Leg of Lamb (page 140).

3 navel oranges

½ teaspoon ground cumin

½ teaspoon kosher salt

½ teaspoon freshly ground black pepper

½ cup peanut or vegetable oil

2 bunches watercress (about 12 ounces)

½ cup crumbled Roquefort or other blue cheese (about 2 ounces)

½ small red onion, peeled and very thinly sliced

1. Cut away the peel and white pith from the oranges using a small knife. Leave as much of the orange intact as possible. Working over a bowl to catch the juice, cut out the orange segments and let them drop into the bowl. After you've cut out all the segments, squeeze the juice from the membrane into the bowl. When you're finished, drain the segments, reserving the juice, and set them aside in the refrigerator.

2. Combine 3 tablespoons of the orange juice, the cumin, salt, and pepper in a blender. Blend well. Add the oil slowly with the motor running and continue blending for 10 seconds. Pour the dressing into a small container with a tight-fitting lid and store in the refrigerator until ready to use.

3. Pick over the watercress, removing any thick stems and wilted or discolored leaves. Wash and dry the sprigs in a salad spinner. Combine the watercress, Roquefort, and red onion in a large bowl and refrigerate until needed. *The salad can be prepared to this point up to 4 hours in advance.*

4. To serve, add the orange segments to the bowl. Shake the dressing well and pour over the salad. Toss gently to mix. Serve immediately.

Curried Vegetable and Apple Salad

Makes 4 servings

When we do an informal buffet, we use simple white platters and bowls and let the food do the talking. This salad, with its vibrant colors and flavors, is very well suited to this treatment. We often serve it with roasted chicken or beef tenderloin.

¼ cup vegetable oil

1 teaspoon curry powder, preferably Madras

2 tablespoons fresh lime juice

2 tablespoons apple juice

2 tablespoons yogurt

2 teaspoons honey

1 teaspoon kosher salt

½ cup raisins

1 large or 2 small carrots, peeled

1 rib celery, very thinly sliced on the bias

1½ cups cut-up cooked vegetables, such as potato, broccoli, or peas

1 Granny Smith apple, quartered, cored, and cut into ½-inch chunks

(continued)

1.   Combine the oil and curry powder in a small skillet over low heat. Heat just until the curry powder begins to give off an aroma, about 1 minute. Scrape into a small bowl and beat in the lime juice, apple juice, yogurt, honey, and salt. Beat until smooth. Add the raisins and toss to coat. Let stand for 15 to 30 minutes.

2.   Cut the carrots into thin julienne strips, either in a food processor or by hand, or coarsely grate them. Add the carrots and celery to the dressing. Add the vegetables and apple to the dressing and toss until coated. Let stand at room temperature for 30 minutes before serving. *The salad may be prepared entirely up to 1 day in advance and stored in the refrigerator. Bring to room temperature and check the seasonings before serving.*

Note: For a main-course salad, substitute 1½ cups of cooked shrimp or chicken for the cooked vegetables.

Blue Collar Potato Salad

Makes 12 servings

Down with New Age potato salad made with firm potatoes! This is one of Blue Collar Food's most requested recipes. There are only two secrets: One, cook the potatoes long enough but not too long—they should be completely tender but still hold their shape—and two, let the salad sit for at least a couple of hours. We make it a day ahead.

2½ pounds waxy potatoes, peeled and cut into ¾-inch dice

1 cup mayonnaise

2 ribs celery, finely diced

1 small red onion, finely diced

¼ cup chopped fresh parsley

1 tablespoon red wine vinegar

1 tablespoon chopped fresh dill

1 tablespoon grainy mustard

1. Place the potatoes in a pot of cold salted water. Bring to a boil over high heat and boil until tender but still firm, about 10 minutes. Drain thoroughly and let cool to room temperature.

2. While the potatoes are cooking, combine the remaining ingredients in a large bowl and stir until blended. Add the potatoes and stir gently until coated with the dressing. The potato salad will taste better if it is refrigerated for at least a few hours before serving. Bring to room temperature about 30 minutes before serving. *The salad is best prepared 1 day ahead; it may be prepared up to 3 days in advance.*

Fruit Cup Ideas

Strawberry and Cantaloupe

Hull strawberries, slice them if they are large, and toss them with chunks of ripe cantaloupe. A small handful of finely chopped fresh mint would be nice.

Pink Grapefruit and Papaya

Peel and cut two large pink grapefruits into segments. (See the directions for segmenting oranges in Step 1 of the recipe for Watercress, Roquefort, and Orange Salad, page 86). Toss in a bowl with one papaya, peeled and sliced. Reserve some of the papaya seeds and top each serving with a few.

Pineapple, Kiwi, and Tangerine

Cut a peeled pineapple into chunks. Toss in a bowl with peeled and sliced kiwifruit and peeled tangerines, pulled apart into segments. Sprinkle the fruit with toasted sesame seeds and oriental sesame oil.

Pineapple-Orange Fruit Cup

Makes 6 servings

Remember fruit cups? Bad memories to the contrary notwithstanding, we still like fruit as a first course. This simple combination of semitropical fruits is a great meal opener, especially one with a lot of spicy flavors, like Curry in a Hurry (page 160) or Grilled Chili-rubbed Flank Steak (page 136).

1 large pineapple

3 navel oranges

12 leaves fresh mint

½ teaspoon finely chopped peeled fresh gingerroot

1. Carefully cut the top and bottom off the pineapple. Cut the pineapple lengthwise in quarters, then cut each quarter in half lengthwise. If desired, cut away the center core from each wedge. Cut the pineapple away from the skin, then cut the pineapple into 1-inch cubes. Place in a large bowl.

2. Cut away the peel and the white pith from the oranges using a small sharp knife. Leave as much of the orange intact as possible. Working over the bowl, cut out the orange segments and let them drop into the bowl. Squeeze the juice from the membrane into the bowl. Tear the leaves of mint and add to the fruit. Add the chopped ginger. Toss well and let stand for 30 minutes before serving. *The salad can be prepared up to 4 hours in advance and stored in the refrigerator. Serve chilled or let stand at room temperature before serving.*

This is one of our favorite summer dishes, best served at room temperature about an hour after it's made. When it's available, we add a large pinch of chopped fresh sage and/or diced roasted yellow pepper. Although generally speaking we have no objection to using canned beans, we feel freshly cooked dried beans are needed here.

5 ounces Great Northern or baby lima beans (¾ cup)

Kosher salt

2 tablespoons olive oil

½ cup thinly sliced celery, including leaves

½ cup very thinly sliced red onion

One 6⅛-ounce can albacore tuna packed in olive oil

1 ripe small tomato, cored and diced

2 tablespoons finely chopped fresh parsley

2 tablespoons fresh lemon juice

Freshly ground black pepper

1. Soak the beans and cook them as described on page 212. After 20 minutes, add about 1 tablespoon salt. Cook until the beans are tender but still firm, about 30 minutes. Drain the beans and transfer them to a large bowl.

2. Add the olive oil and toss until the beans are coated. Add the celery, onion, tuna, tomato, parsley, and lemon juice. Season to taste with salt and pepper, and toss to mix. Let the salad stand at room temperature for 30 minutes to 1 hour before serving. *The salad may be made up to 1 day ahead. Bring to room temperature 30 minutes before serving and check the seasoning.*

Pasta

Pasta is a boom that knows no bust.
How come? The explanation is
simple: It's Blue Collar food—
cheap, no fuss, and endlessly
versatile. Pasta can be dressed
up with crab and tomato or
prosciutto and peas for company;
it can be thrown together in
a trice with some fried garlic or
canned tuna for a solo supper after work.

As professional chefs, we've developed countless pasta sauces for
menu items and daily specials over the years. In a busy restaurant kitchen, such
pasta dishes must be simple and quick to prepare——exactly what the busy home
cook is looking for too.

The inspiration for our recipes comes from childhood memories, work
and travel experiences, and our own instincts. We've both worked and traveled in
Italy, where the seasons and ingredients at hand shape each day's sauce. And
we've cooked in American restaurant kitchens with some of our generation's most

creative chefs, who, we can assure you, do not disdain a well-made plate of pasta.

Pasta is at its optimum when freshly made and sauced and served straight from the pot. Most of our dishes fit that description, and the sauces can be made in the time it takes to boil the water and cook the pasta al dente. For occasions that don't allow for such split-second timing, we offer several baked pasta dishes and pasta salads. These are top sellers on our catering menu; they are particularly well suited to informal entertaining.

Pantry Pastas

Pasta is so quick, so easy to prepare that with a little strategic planning you need never go without a satisfying supper, no matter how tired or pressed for time you think you are. Even when the cupboard looks bare, something's probably lurking in there that you can use to dress spaghetti, if only a couple of cloves of garlic. Ideally, though, your pantry will always be stocked with the following:

- An assortment of dried pasta shapes, mainly strands like spaghetti, spaghettini, linguine, and so on.
- A chunk of parmesan cheese for grating or shaving.
- Fresh garlic, red onion, and parsley.
- Olive oil, good tasting but not necessarily top dollar.
- Cans of solid white tuna, anchovy fillets (or anchovy paste), and plum tomatoes, both small and large size cans.
- European green and black olives, oil cured and/or packed in brine.
- Capers, packed in vinegar brine or, if you're lucky enough to find them, under salt.
- Dried herbs (basil, oregano, tarragon) and crushed red pepper.
- Dried breadcrumbs.

With these staples on hand, you can throw together a pasta dish in minutes, either by following one of our recipes or giving your imagination full rein. We've also included three of our basic sauce recipes—two tomato sauces, which can be made in quantity and refrigerated or frozen for future use, and an unusual lowfat pesto that can be refrigerated for a couple of days, though it's best freshly made.

Tomato Sauce

Makes 7 cups

We've never understood why anyone would buy commercial pasta sauce when it's so easy to make your own. And so much better! For this sauce, which takes about forty-five minutes start to finish, we use imported canned San Marzano tomatoes, which are sold under several brand names. Check the label for a mention of San Marzano. These tomatoes are pleasantly acidic, as close in taste to fresh tomatoes as you can get. This is a basic sauce, which you can use as is on pasta and in other dishes. Or you can doctor it with additional herbs, like oregano, bay leaf, fennel seed, or fresh basil, as you see fit. One cup of sauce is enough for two servings.

Two 28-ounce cans Italian-style plum tomatoes, with their liquid
¼ cup extra virgin olive oil
2 cloves garlic, finely chopped
2 tablespoons chopped fresh parsley
1 teaspoon kosher salt
¼ teaspoon freshly ground black pepper

Blend the tomatoes, 1 can at a time, at low speed until smooth. Return each batch of puree to the can. Heat the olive oil in a medium heavy saucepan over medium heat. Add the garlic and parsley. Sauté until you can smell the garlic, 1 minute or less. Immediately begin to slowly add the tomato. Bring to a boil, reduce the heat, stir in the salt and pepper, and simmer, stirring occasionally, until the sauce is thickened, 35 to 40 minutes. Check the seasoning. *The sauce may be made up to 3 days in advance and refrigerated or frozen for up to 3 months.*

How to Cook Pasta

If you can boil water, you can cook pasta. Start by pouring a lot of water into a large pot. For ¾ pound of pasta (enough for 3 or 4 servings), we recommend 3 quarts of water in a 5- to 6-quart pot; anything smaller, the pot is likely to boil over when you add the pasta. Throw in at least 2 tablespoons of kosher salt, cover the pot, and bring to a vigorous boil over high heat. Don't skimp on the salt—pasta doesn't cook right or taste right without plenty of it. As soon as you've put the pot on the stove, set a colander in the sink.

Add the pasta to the boiling water and stir it immediately. Stir all pasta shapes several times during the first 2 minutes; stir long ones constantly until they are soft enough to bend easily. After the first couple of minutes, stir the pasta 2 or 3 times. Leave the heat on high—the sooner the water returns to a boil and the harder it boils the better. We never add oil or anything other than salt to the water. All you need to keep pasta from sticking is plenty of water and sufficient stirring.

Taste the pasta from time to time to see if it's done. It should be slightly undercooked if it is to be cooked again, as in a baked dish. Otherwise, we like our pasta al dente. This is an Italian phrase that means cooked just long enough to remain firm with a bit of bite and a pleasant nutty flavor but no raw pasta taste. We don't give cooking times in our recipes, not even approximate ones, because they vary so much from brand to brand. When the pasta is almost done, ladle out 1 cup of the cooking water to use if needed to thin the sauce.

Drain the pasta when it is cooked to your liking. Grab two potholders, tip the pot over the colander, and slowly pour off the water, letting the pasta settle into the bottom of the pot. (Avert your face and keep your hands out of the steam. Steam burns are among the worst you can get in the kitchen.) Dump the pasta into the colander and shake out as much water as you can, especially from hollow shapes like penne and rigatoni. Don't rinse the pasta unless you are going to cook it again or make a cold pasta dish.

Return the drained pasta to the pot and add the sauce, tossing to coat. (This gives the pasta a head start on absorbing the sauce and seasonings.) If the sauce seems too thick or there's not enough of it, add some of the reserved cooking water, a little at a time, until the sauce is thin enough to coat the pasta. Add any last-minute ingredients like grated cheese or chopped herbs, toss again, and check the seasoning.

Transfer the pasta to a large platter or serve it directly from the pot into individual shallow bowls or plates. It helps to warm the bowls before serving. Eat right away.

Chunky Fresh Plum Tomato Sauce

Makes 4 cups

This is the sauce to make in late summer and early fall when plum tomatoes flood the roadside stands and farmers' markets. We give amounts to make four cups (allow one cup for four servings of pasta), but you really ought to make more when you can. Freeze it in small containers for the ultimate in no-fuss afterwork cooking year-round. Bill once brought his mother-in-law a gallon of the stuff, and she said it was "like Christmas morning." This sauce is good with just about any kind of pasta.

¼ cup olive oil

2 cloves garlic, finely chopped

1 tablespoon chopped Italian (flat-leaf) parsley

4 pounds ripe plum tomatoes, peeled and seeded (page 68)

2 tablespoons chopped fresh basil or 2 teaspoons dried basil

½ teaspoon kosher salt

¼ teaspoon freshly ground black pepper

Heat the olive oil in a medium heavy saucepan over medium heat. Add the garlic and parsley. Sauté until you can smell the garlic, 1 minute or less. Immediately begin to slowly add the tomatoes. Bring to a boil, reduce the heat, cover, and simmer, stirring occasionally, for 20 minutes. Uncover, add the basil, salt, and pepper and cook until the sauce is slightly thickened, about 25 minutes. Stir the tomatoes and mash them with a spoon during the cooking to make a sauce of chunky consistency. Check the seasoning. *The sauce may be made up to 3 days in advance and refrigerated or frozen for up to 2 months.*

Cottage Cheese and Spinach Pesto

Makes 1⅓ cups, enough for 4 servings

This is a good low-calorie alternative to traditional pesto. It looks great and delivers a fresh green flavor without the oil and nuts. And unlike basil, spinach is available at a good price all year long, so you can prepare it whenever you like. Use it on spaghetti, linguine, or penne. We recommend sprinkling the pasta generously with grated parmesan and accompanying the dish with our Tomato-Feta Salad with Fresh Dill (page 83).

½ pound loose or half 10-ounce cellophane pack fresh spinach, stemmed, washed, and dried

½ cup lowfat cottage cheese

3 tablespoons water

Kosher salt

Freshly ground black pepper

Combine the spinach, cottage cheese, and water in a food processor and process until the spinach is very finely chopped. Stop the machine to scrape down the sides once or twice. Or prepare the sauce in a blender: Coarsely chop the spinach. Puree the cottage cheese and water in the blender and add the spinach in batches. Stop often to scrape down the sides of the jar. Season to taste with salt and pepper. *The pesto may be prepared up to 3 days in advance and refrigerated. Bring back to room temperature before serving.*

This is our take on the Neapolitan classic spaghetti con olio e aglio. The trick is to season the oil with garlic, removing it the minute it begins to brown. The simple flavors of the dish are addictive. Ask Gary Maurer, Blue Collar's "Dean of Delivery." He lives on it for days at a time.

¼ cup olive oil

4 cloves garlic, thinly sliced

Pinch crushed red pepper

2 tablespoons chopped fresh parsley or fresh basil

¾ pound spaghetti, spaghettini, or linguine

¼ cup grated parmesan, plus more for passing

1 teaspoon kosher salt

Pinch freshly ground black pepper

1. Heat the oil in a small heavy skillet over low heat. Add the garlic slices and fry them just until they begin to turn brown around the edges, 2 to 3 minutes. Immediately remove the garlic with a slotted spoon and set aside. Act as soon as you see a slice start to change color, once the garlic starts to brown it can burn very quickly. Turn off the heat and add the crushed red pepper and parsley to the oil. Set aside. *The oil can be prepared to this point up to 2 hours in advance.*

2. Cook the spaghetti in a large pot of boiling salted water until al dente. Measure out and reserve 1 cup of the pasta cooking liquid. Meanwhile, reheat the oil if necessary. Drain the pasta in a colander and return to the pot. Add the seasoned oil, garlic, ¼ cup of parmesan, and ¼ cup of the reserved pasta cooking liquid. Add the salt and pepper and stir until the spaghetti is coated with sauce. Add more cooking liquid if necessary to coat the pasta. Check the seasonings and transfer to a serving platter or individual plates. Serve immediately, passing additional parmesan separately.

We picked up this recipe while working with the <u>monzù</u> chef Mario Lo Menzo in Sicily. When the tuna is running——it's still abundant in those waters——Signor Mario always packs some in olive oil to have on hand the rest of the year. We tried this dish with canned tuna, with excellent results. We never say never, but in Sicily they insist you should <u>never</u> put grated cheese on fish; they use toasted breadcrumbs instead.

¼ cup dried breadcrumbs

¼ cup olive oil, preferably extra virgin

½ small red onion, finely chopped

1 clove garlic, finely chopped

2 tablespoons chopped fresh parsley

Two 6⅛-ounce cans tuna in vegetable or olive oil, rinsed and drained

⅔ cup Tomato Sauce (page 95) or canned tomato sauce, or pasta
    cooking liquid (see Note)

2 tablespoons capers, rinsed and drained (optional)

¼ teaspoon kosher salt

¼ teaspoon freshly ground black pepper

¾ pound linguine, spaghettini, or spaghetti

1. Stir the breadcrumbs in a small skillet over medium-high heat until golden brown, about 3 minutes. Remove from the heat and set aside.

2. Heat the oil in a small heavy saucepan over medium heat. Add the onion and stir until it begins to brown, 3 to 5 minutes. Add the garlic and parsley and sauté for 1 minute. Add the tuna. Stir in the tomato sauce, capers, if using, salt, and pepper. *The sauce may be prepared to this point up to 1 day in advance and refrigerated.*

(continued)

Pasta

3. Cook the linguine in a large pot of boiling salted water until al dente. Meanwhile, reheat the sauce if necessary. Drain in a colander and return it to the pot. Pour the sauce on the pasta and toss to coat. Check the seasonings and transfer the pasta to a serving platter or individual plates. Sprinkle about half the breadcrumbs over the pasta and pass the remaining crumbs separately.

Note: For a different type of dish or if you are making this on the spur of the moment, use some of the pasta cooking liquid to replace the tomato sauce. Ladle ⅓ cup of the liquid into the tuna mixture in Step 2 and heat to a boil.

Pasta Puttanesca from the Pantry

Makes 4 servings

It is said this dish originated among the ladies of the night in Naples. (Does that make it the world's oldest pasta dish?) Like most working girls, they were looking for a quick, inexpensive, and easy-to-prepare meal, and this zesty sauce could be made in minutes straight from the pantry shelf. If the ingredients aren't on yours, you ought to put them there to be ready for an emergency dinner.

2 tablespoons olive oil

3 cloves garlic, finely chopped

Crushed red pepper

One 16-ounce can plum tomatoes, coarsely chopped, with their liquid

¾ pound penne, rigatoni, or fusilli (corkscrews)

¼ cup chopped fresh parsley or 2 teaspoons dried basil

3 tablespoons chopped pitted green or black olives (about 6–12 olives, depending on size)

4 to 6 anchovy fillets, chopped, or 4–6 inches anchovy paste from a
    tube
1 tablespoon capers (optional)
Kosher salt
Freshly ground black pepper
Grated parmesan or romano

1. Heat the oil in a large skillet over medium heat. Add the garlic and red pepper to taste and sauté until the garlic is fragrant, about 30 seconds. Carefully add the tomatoes to the skillet. Bring the sauce to a boil, reduce the heat, and simmer uncovered, for 15 minutes. *The sauce may be prepared to this point up to 2 days in advance.*

2. Cook the penne in a large pot of boiling salted water until al dente. Meanwhile, stir the parsley, olives, anchovies, and capers into the sauce and simmer for 5 minutes. Check the seasoning and add salt and pepper if necessary.

3. Drain the pasta well and return it to the pot. Add the sauce and stir until the pasta is coated. Transfer the pasta to a serving platter or individual bowls and serve at once. Pass the grated cheese separately.

As a rule, pasta is not good party food since timing is of the essence. The pasta must be cooked just so; it has to be sauced as soon as it's done; and the dish should be eaten the minute it's ready. That's all right as long as there's someone in the kitchen to perform the sacred ritual while the others sit in their pews waiting to be served. Hardly a contemporary picture. Not to mention the case of casual stand-up parties where twirling long strands of sauce-coated pasta from plates held in the air or, at best, on the knees defeats even the most adroit.

We considered it a challenge to find pasta dishes we could serve at parties. In this section we present some dishes that have worked well for us. The first is a sit-down dish as described above, but crab is so festive and luxurious we feel it should be on the menu for special occasions. The other dishes all involve cooking the pasta twice, either warming it in a stovetop sauce or baking it in a casserole. For these dishes, the pasta must be one of the hollow types, like penne, rigatoni, or fusilli (corkscrews) which stand up to long cooking. An added advantage of baked pasta for entertaining is that it can be made in advance and frozen until needed. In fact, if you are making such a dish just for yourself—or for you and your loved one—we suggest you freeze the extra portions for another time.

When we serve baked pasta at a buffet party, we always put a big salad or two out near it. It never fails to amaze us how much people appreciate this kind of food. Maybe it's because they can understand it without calling for an interpreter.

Because of our training and experience, we tend to lean on technique to bring out flavor. In this dish there's no place to hide—it's only fresh crab and ripe tomato—so we infuse the oil with garlic. It leaves enough of an aroma to perfume the entire dish.

½ pound lump or backfin crab meat (see Note)

3 tablespoons olive oil

1 clove garlic, cut in half

¼ cup chopped fresh parsley

1 ripe medium tomato, cored and diced

Kosher salt

Freshly ground black pepper

¾ pound spaghettini or fine linguine

1. Pick over the crab meat to remove any pieces of shell or cartilage. Keep refrigerated until ready to make the sauce.

2. Heat the oil and garlic over medium-low heat until the garlic is golden brown on all sides, about 3 minutes. Turn the garlic once or twice so it browns evenly. Remove the garlic pieces with a slotted spoon and discard them. Add 2 tablespoons of the parsley and fry for 10 seconds. Carefully slide the tomato into the pan. Cook until the tomato is very tender, about 2 minutes. Add salt and pepper to taste. Stir the crab meat into the sauce and set the sauce aside. *The sauce can be prepared to this point up to 2 hours in advance.*

3. Cook the spaghettini in a large pot of boiling salted water until al dente. Drain well and return it to the pot. Add the sauce and stir until the pasta is

(continued)

Pasta

105

coated with sauce and heated through. Check the seasoning and add more salt and pepper if necessary. Transfer the pasta to a serving platter or individual plates, top with the remaining parsley, and serve immediately.

Note: Other types of crab meat can be substituted for the lump or backfin—stone crab, king crab, or dungeness crab meat to name a few. Try to find freshly cooked meat from fresh crabs, using canned or frozen crab meat only as a last resort.

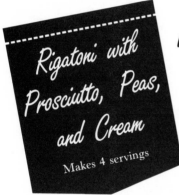

Rigatoni with Prosciutto, Peas, and Cream

Makes 4 servings

We believe good food—like this menu staple of the 1970s— never goes out of style. Be sure to undercook the pasta somewhat since it will continue to cook in the sauce. Precede or follow the dish with a green salad.

¾ cup heavy cream

¼ pound mushrooms, trimmed and sliced

¼ pound thinly sliced prosciutto, cut into thin strips

10 ounces rigatoni (4 cups)

1 cup frozen peas, defrosted (See Note)

1 tablespoon chopped fresh or dried chives

Kosher salt

Freshly ground black pepper

⅔ cup grated parmesan

1. Combine the cream, mushrooms, and prosciutto in a small skillet. Bring to a boil over medium heat. Boil until the liquid is slightly thickened, about 2 minutes. Be careful it doesn't boil over. *The sauce may be prepared to this point up to 1 day in advance. Store covered in the refrigerator. Heat to simmering over low heat before continuing with the recipe.*

2. Cook the pasta in a large pot of boiling salted water until al dente. Drain and return the pasta to the pot and add the cream mixture, peas, and chives. Heat to boiling while stirring the pasta to coat with the sauce. Add salt and pepper to taste and 3 tablespoons of the parmesan. Transfer the pasta to a serving platter or individual plates. Pass the remaining parmesan.

Note: You may substitute 1 cup shelled fresh peas in season for the frozen peas. Blanch the peas in boiling salted water for 1 to 2 minutes, drain, and rinse under cold water, draining thoroughly. You may also substitute 1 cup thinly sliced sugar snap peas or snow peas. Blanch the sugar snap peas as you would fresh peas. Snow peas need no blanching.

Penne with Chicken, Asparagus, and Dried Tomatoes

Makes 4 servings

We OD'd on dried tomatoes a couple of years ago and still tend to shy away from them. But here their intense flavor adds real depth to a light broth-based sauce. Since the pasta will be reheated in the sauce, we rinse it under cold water to stop the cooking. This is one of those rare dishes where you can prepare the pasta in advance and quickly throw the sauce together at the last minute.

½ pound penne (2 cups)

1 tablespoon olive oil

1 clove garlic, minced

½ teaspoon dried rosemary

½-pound skinless chicken cutlet, trimmed of fat and cut into ¼-inch dice

12 thin spears asparagus, trimmed and thinly sliced

10 dried tomatoes, cut into thin strips (see Note)

½ cup Chicken Broth, preferably homemade (page 53), or low-sodium canned broth

½ cup grated parmesan

2 tablespoons chopped fresh parsley

Kosher salt

Freshly ground black pepper

1. Cook the pasta in a pot of boiling salted water until al dente. Drain and rinse under cold running water until cool. Drain thoroughly. *Pasta may be prepared to this point up to 6 hours in advance.*

2. Heat the olive oil in a large deep skillet over medium heat. Add the garlic and rosemary and cook for 15 seconds. Stir in the chicken and asparagus and toss in the oil until the chicken is lightly browned, about 3 minutes. Add the dried tomatoes, broth, and pasta. Increase the heat to high and scrape up the bits sticking to the pan. Let the sauce boil, tossing all the ingredients occasionally, until the liquid is thickened enough to lightly coat the pasta. Add 2 tablespoons of the parmesan, parsley, and salt and pepper to taste. Serve at once, passing the remaining parmesan.

Note: To keep the dish lowfat and economical, use plain dried tomatoes and soak them in hot water until soft. It's not necessary to use dried tomatoes that have been reconstituted and packed in olive oil.

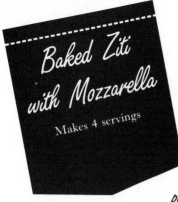

You can build on the simple base of this dish by adding other ingredients—lightly cooked broccoli, sautéed mushrooms, leftover chicken, and the like. We've even crumbled the last of a Turkey Meat Loaf (page 148) into the mix. We use fresh mozzarella, which has become far more widely available than it used to be. The flavor is much better than that of packaged mozzarella, but it isn't as stringy. You might be happier with a mix of the two. If you can't get the fresh, by all means use the packaged—this dish is too good to deny yourself the pleasure. Just be sure to reduce the amount of salt.

¾ pound cut ziti, penne, or penne rigate (3 cups)

2 cups Tomato Sauce (page 95)

¾ pound mozzarella, preferably fresh, grated (1½ cups)

⅓ cup grated parmesan

1 tablespoon chopped fresh basil

1 teaspoon kosher salt

¼ teaspoon freshly ground black pepper

1. Cook the pasta in a large pot of boiling salted water until al dente; it should be slightly underdone. Drain the pasta, rinse under cold running water, and drain thoroughly, shaking the colander well to remove as much water as possible. Transfer the pasta to a large mixing bowl. Adding the remaining ingredients, reserving ½ cup each of the tomato sauce and mozzarella. Toss all the ingredients well. Transfer to an 8 × 8-inch baking dish. Top with the remaining sauce, then the cheese. *The pasta may be prepared to this point up to 1 day in advance. Bring to room temperature for at least 30 minutes before baking. The pasta may also be frozen in the baking dish. Defrost in the refrigerator for 1 day before baking.*

2.   Heat the oven to 350°F.

3.   For a creamy consistency, bake just until the center is heated through, about 30 minutes. For a firmer consistency, continue baking until the top is golden brown, about 15 minutes more. Let stand 5 minutes before serving.

Except for the pork, which you could easily omit, this dish can be made entirely from pantry staples. Although we cook beans a lot at Blue Collar Food, we think everyone deserves a break once in a while. Canned beans are perfectly OK in this dish.

½ pound fusilli (corkscrews), ziti, or penne (2 cups)

¼ pound very lean ground pork

1 small onion, diced

1 rib celery, trimmed and finely diced

¼ teaspoon dried sage

One 16-ounce can tomatoes, liquid reserved, finely chopped

1½ cups Chicken Broth, preferably homemade (page 53), or low-sodium canned broth or water

One 15½-ounce can white beans (cannellini), rinsed and drained

Kosher salt

Freshly ground black pepper

2 tablespoons dried breadcrumbs

2 tablespoons grated parmesan

1. Heat the oven to 350°F. Cook the pasta in a large pot of boiling salted water until slightly undercooked. Drain and rinse until cold running water until cool. Drain thoroughly, shaking the colander to remove all water.

2. Crumble the pork into a medium skillet and place over medium heat. Cook, stirring occasionally, until the pork is cooked through, about 4 minutes.

3. Pour off all but 1 tablespoon of the drippings in the skillet. Add the onion, celery, and sage. Cook until the vegetables are softened, about 3 minutes. Add the tomatoes and bring to a boil, scraping the bottom of the skillet. Boil for 3 minutes.

4. Transfer the contents of the skillet to a mixing bowl. Add the broth, beans, and salt and pepper to taste. Stir well.

5. Transfer the mixture to an 8 × 8-inch baking dish. Mix the bread-crumbs and parmesan in a small bowl and sprinkle over the casserole. Bake until heated through in the center and the breadcrumb mixture is golden brown, about 20 minutes. Let stand 5 minutes before serving.

Note: You may divide the mixture in half in Step 5, freezing half and baking the other. Choose 2 baking dishes in which half the pasta and bean mixture will make a layer about 1½ inches deep. Or freeze the entire amount. Defrost in the refrigerator for 1 day before baking.

Baked Shells with Broccoli and Blue Cheese

Makes 4 servings

Not everyone likes broccoli and not everyone likes blue cheese, but we love them both and have created this dish for those of you who share our cravings. We fully expect the food police to read us the riot act on that can of cream of broccoli soup. We are prepared to take the case all the way to the Supreme Court, trusting they will not deem it frivolous. The stuff in the can makes a superlative sauce for this unusual baked pasta dish.

¾ pound medium shell pasta (3 cups)

One 10½-ounce can cream of broccoli soup

¾ cup milk

2 cups finely chopped broccoli florets

⅓ cup (loosely packed) Danish or domestic blue cheese, crumbled (2 ounces)

2 teaspoons olive oil

½ cup plus 2 tablespoons dried breadcrumbs

Kosher salt

Freshly ground black pepper

1. Cook the pasta in a large pot of boiling salted water until slightly undercooked. Drain the pasta, rinse it under cold running water and drain thoroughly, shaking out the water.

2. Heat the soup and milk to simmering in a small saucepan over medium heat, stirring once or twice. Remove the pan from the heat. Add the broccoli and cheese and stir until the cheese is melted.

3. Heat the oven to 375°F.

4. Grease an 8 × 8-inch baking dish with the olive oil. Coat the bottom and sides of the dish with ½ cup of the breadcrumbs. Combine the pasta and soup mixture in a bowl and stir until the pasta is coated with sauce. Check the seasoning and add salt, if necessary, and pepper to taste. Turn the pasta into the prepared baking dish. Top with the remaining 2 tablespoons of breadcrumbs. *The pasta may be prepared to this point and refrigerated up to 1 day in advance. Bring to room temperature for 30 minutes before baking.*

5. Bake until the sauce is bubbling around the edges and the top is golden brown, about 30 minutes. Let stand 5 minutes before serving.

From its origins as a *primo piatto,* or first dish, in Italy, pasta has come to be considered a main course in America, at home at least. But there are some pasta dishes that don't quite make entrée level. We have grouped three of them here.

Stir-fried Curried Pasta

Makes 6 first-course servings

We like to fool around combining tastes and techniques from different culinary traditions. Frankly, it doesn't always work, but sometimes, as in this inspired dish, the mix clicks. The colors are spectacular; the flavors are in perfect harmony. As with most stir-fry dishes, advance preparation takes a bit of time, but you catch up in the cooking, which goes very fast. Read the recipe carefully before embarking.

1½ cups medium shell pasta (6 ounces)

½ pound loose or half 10-ounce cellophane pack fresh spinach

2 tablespoons peanut oil or vegetable oil

3 scallions, thinly sliced on the bias

2 teaspoons minced peeled fresh gingerroot

1 teaspoon curry powder, preferably Madras

1 clove garlic, minced

18 medium shrimp, peeled and deveined (about 1 pound)

¾ pound ripe plum tomatoes, cored, seeded, and cut into ¼-inch dice

¼ cup plain lowfat yogurt

¼ cup Chicken Broth, preferably homemade (page 53), or low-sodium
   canned broth

Kosher salt

1. Cook the shells in a large amount of boiling salted water, stirring frequently, until the shells are al dente. Drain, rinse under cold running water until completely cooled. Drain them thoroughly. Stem the spinach, wash it, and dry well. Shred the leaves ½ inch. *The ingredients may be prepared as called for in the ingredient list and the recipe may be prepared to this point up to 4 hours in advance.*

2. Heat the oil in a wok over high heat, swirling to coat the sides. Add the scallions, ginger, curry powder, and garlic and fry until fragrant, about 10 seconds. Add the shrimp and toss to coat with the seasoned oil. Cook until all the shrimp have changed color, about 1 minute. Add the spinach and stir-fry until it is wilted but still bright green, about 30 seconds. Add the tomatoes and pasta. Toss until the ingredients are evenly distributed throughout the pasta. Add the yogurt and broth and toss until the pasta is coated with the sauce. Cover the wok and boil until the pasta is heated through, about 30 seconds. Taste and add salt if necessary. Transfer the pasta to individual bowls or plates and serve immediately.

Orzo is a rice-shaped pasta, usually cooked al dente in a lot of water or broth. We have found that when it is cooked longer in only as much liquid as it can absorb, the orzo behaves like rice and turns into a quasi pilaf or risotto, as in this dish. When we were home-testing recipes for this book, we sent some, including this one, to family and friends living in different parts of the country. We wanted to check if certain ingredients were generally available, if our techniques were clearly explained, and if our ideas were appealing. This dish, though unusual, turned out to be one of the most popular.

1½ cups Chicken Broth, preferably homemade (page 53), or low-sodium canned broth

1 medium russet potato, peeled and cut into ½-inch dice

1 teaspoon kosher salt

Large pinch freshly ground black pepper

1 pound broccoli rabe, stemmed and coarsely chopped (about 3 cups)

6 ounces orzo (1 cup)

2 tablespoons grated parmesan

Combine the broth, potato, salt, and pepper in a medium heavy-bottomed saucepan. Bring to a boil over medium heat and boil, covered, for 3 minutes. Add the broccoli rabe and orzo and stir well until the liquid returns to the boil. Reduce the heat to low and simmer for 2 to 3 minutes, scraping the bottom of the pan continuously with a flat wooden spoon or metal spatula. Cover the pan and simmer until the orzo and potato are tender and enough of the liquid is absorbed to make a creamy sauce, about 10 minutes. Uncover the pan several times and stir well, making sure the orzo doesn't stick to the sides or bottom of the pan. If the liquid is absorbed before the pasta is tender, add cold water, 1 tablespoon at a time, as necessary. Remove the pan from the heat and stir in the parmesan. Check the seasoning and serve immediately.

Note: Broccoli rabe, sometimes marketed as rapini, is a somewhat bitter green, which looks like a loose leaf broccoli. If you don't find broccoli rabe in your market, substitute 3 cups chopped broccoli florets.

Angel Hair Pancakes

Makes two 6-inch pancakes

We never tire of pasta, and we are always looking for new ways to serve it. These versatile crisp pancakes were a revelation. They can be served hot or at room temperature, as a first course topped with a salad of tender greens or as a side dish with grilled lamb or chicken. During a stint of cheffing, Bill even served them for brunch.

¼ pound dried angel hair pasta

1 egg

¼ cup grated parmesan

¼ cup diced roasted red pepper or diced cooked broccoli (see Note)

½ teaspoon kosher salt

Pinch freshly ground black pepper

¼ cup breadcrumbs

2 tablespoons olive oil

1. Cook the pasta in a large pot of boiling salted water until tender. Drain and rinse under cold running water until cool. Drain thoroughly.

2. Combine the egg, cheese, roasted red pepper, and salt and pepper in a large mixing bowl and beat until blended. Mix the pasta into the egg mixture with your hands until all the pasta is coated. Mix the breadcrumbs into the mixture in the same way. Let the mixture stand at room temperature for 30 minutes to 1 hour.

3. If you are serving the pasta pancakes hot, heat the oven to 250°F.

4. Pour 1 tablespoon of the oil into a 6-inch nonstick skillet and place the skillet over medium heat. Let the oil heat until it becomes thinner and coats the bottom of the skillet easily. Measure 1 cup of the pasta mixture and add it to the skillet. Flatten the pasta into an even layer with the back of a large spoon or a spatula.

Cook the pancake, shaking the skillet occasionally, until the underside is golden brown and crisp, about 3 minutes. Carefully flip the pancake and continue cooking until the second side is golden brown, about 3 minutes. If you are serving the pancakes hot, slide the first pancake onto a baking sheet and place it in the oven while preparing the second pancake. If you are serving the pancakes at room temperature, slide the pancake onto a cutting surface. Heat the remaining oil and make a second pancake with the remaining pasta mixture. Cut each pancake into 4 wedges before serving.

Note: Substitute peas, chopped mushrooms, or very thinly sliced string beans (all cooked) for the peppers or broccoli.

Room-Temperature Pasta Dishes

Having eaten more than our share of bland, soggy, gummy pasta salads from delis and take-out shops, we were determined from Day One that ours would be properly cooked, well seasoned, and fresh tasting. We experimented until we found a way that guarantees perfect pasta salads every time. This is what we recommend:

Cook the pasta al dente as described on page 96. (Unlike strands, small pasta shapes when cooked al dente are actually slightly underdone and better able to withstand chilling and standing.) Drain the pasta and rinse it well under cold running water, tossing it in the colander, until it is thoroughly chilled. Shake the colander to remove as much water as possible.

While the pasta is cooking, make the dressing in a bowl. Add the pasta and toss until all the pasta is coated. If olive oil is called for in the recipe instead of dressing, add it and toss the pasta to coat. Add the remaining ingredients and toss until they are evenly distributed.

If possible, make the dish shortly before serving and let it stand for about about 30 minutes. Taste it and correct the seasonings, toss again, and serve at room temperature.

Refrigerate only if necessary and for no more than 6 hours—refrigeration hurts the texture and flavor of most pasta salads. Remove the pasta salad from the refrigerator at least 30 minutes before serving and let it come to room temperature. Be sure to taste and correct the seasoning if necessary. If the pasta is stuck together, add hot water, 1 tablespoon at a time, to "unstick" it.

Tomato, Basil, and Mozzarella Salad with Penne

Makes 4 luncheon or 8 side-dish servings

Serendipity helps. One day we tossed some pasta into a favorite summer salad. Just like that, it worked. Quill-shaped penne is perfect.

½ pound penne or penne rigate (about 2 cups)

3 tablespoons olive oil

¼ pound mozzarella (preferably fresh) diced

2 tablespoons red wine vinegar

¼ cup grated parmesan

4 fresh plum tomatoes, cored, seeded, and diced (about 1 cup)

¼ cup (packed) finely shredded fresh basil

Kosher salt

Freshly ground black pepper

1. Cook the pasta in a large pot of boiling salted water, stirring occasionally, until al dente. Drain well in a colander and rinse under cold running water until cool. Drain very well, shaking the colander to remove as much water as possible.

2. Place the pasta in a bowl. Add the olive oil and toss until the pasta is coated. Add the mozzarella, vinegar, parmesan, tomatoes, and basil to mix. Add salt and pepper to taste and toss again. Let stand for at least 30 minutes at room temperature before serving. Taste just before serving and adjust the seasoning if necessary.

Pasta

Asparagus, Pine Nut, and Shell Pasta Salad

Makes 4 servings

Pine nuts got very chi-chi a couple of years back as chefs started using them with wild abandon. Definitely not a Blue Collar kind of thing to do. In this pasta salad, though, we find a sprinkling of pine nuts adds just the right touch of crunch. You can use chopped almonds or walnuts instead if you like. Just don't omit the nuts altogether.

½ pound medium asparagus (about 12 spears)

¾ pound small shell pasta (about 3 cups)

1 tablespoon balsamic vinegar

1 tablespoon Dijon mustard

1 teaspoon kosher salt

¼ teaspoon freshly ground black pepper

⅓ cup olive oil

2 tablespoons pine nuts (see Note)

2 tablespoons chopped drained pimiento or roasted red pepper (about half 4-ounce jar)

1. Bend each stalk of asparagus until it snaps. Discard the tough lower part. Cut the tips off, then cut the spears on an angle very thin. Blanch the asparagus until they are crisp-tender, about 1 minute. Drain well.

2. Cook the pasta in a large pot of boiling salted water until al dente. Drain the pasta in a colander and rinse under cold water until cool. Drain well, shaking the colander to remove as much water as possible.

3. While the pasta is cooking, combine the vinegar, mustard, salt, and pepper in a bowl. Slowly whisk in the oil to make a smooth dressing. Add the pasta to the dressing and toss to coat. Add the asparagus, pine nuts, and pimiento and toss well. Let the salad stand at room temperature for 30 minutes. Check the seasoning before serving.

Notes: True pine nuts—*pignoli* in Italian—are very costly. Sometimes cheaper Chinese pine kernels are sold as the real thing—which is all right as long as you don't pay top dollar for them.

If you like, toast the pine nuts in a small skillet over low heat, shaking or stirring frequently, until golden brown.

Chicken, Roasted Tomato, and Fusilli Salad

Makes 4 servings

The perfect salad for late summer, when tomatoes and corn are at their peak. Roasting the tomatoes concentrates their flavor and draws off the juice, which could make the salad soggy. Cilantro adds the right herbal touch.

3 tablespoons olive oil plus some for the baking pan

3 ripe large tomatoes (about 1½ pounds)

½ pound fusilli (corkscrews) (about 3 cups)

2 cups shredded or diced cooked chicken (see Note)

½ cup cooked fresh corn kernels or frozen corn, defrosted and drained

2 tablespoons chopped fresh cilantro or parsley

1 tablespoon white wine vinegar

1. Place the oven rack in the highest position and heat the oven to 400°F. Lightly oil a baking pan using some of the olive oil.

2. Core the tomatoes, then cut them in half crosswise through the thickest part. Squeeze out the seeds and place the tomatoes, cut side down, on the baking sheet. Roast until the skins are slightly charred and the tomatoes are very tender, about 20 minutes. Let stand until cool enough to handle. Slip the skins off and leave the tomatoes to drain in a colander. *The salad may be prepared to this point up to 2 hours in advance.*

3. Cook the pasta in a large pot of boiling salted water until al dente. Drain in a colander and rinse it under cold running water until cool. Drain the pasta well, shaking the colander to remove as much water as possible.

4. Transfer the pasta to a bowl and toss with 3 tablespoons of the olive oil until the pasta is coated. Add the chicken, corn, cilantro, and vinegar. Toss to mix. Coarsely chop the roasted tomatoes and add to the salad. Let stand at room temperature for up to 1 hour before serving. Toss again and check the seasonings before serving.

Note: An equal amount of cooked turkey or shrimp may be substituted for the chicken.

Blue Collar Macaroni Salad with Seafood

Makes 4 servings

Unlike the dread macaroni salads of yore, this one knows no mayo. It is lightly dressed to show off the briny bits of seafood. You can prepare the yogurt–sour cream dressing and the seafood ahead of time. Combine them about half an hour before serving.

1 ripe medium tomato

1 pound elbow macaroni or small shell pasta (4 cups)

¼ cup sour cream, regular or lowfat

¼ cup yogurt

¼ cup chopped fresh dill

2 teaspoons kosher salt

¼ teaspoon freshly ground black pepper

1 cup coarsely chopped cooked shrimp, bay scallops, crab meat, or
      salmon, or any mixture

1. Core the tomato and slice it ½ inch thick. Remove as many of the seeds as you can. Cut the tomato into ½-inch dice. Drain in a strainer.

2. Cook the macaroni in a large pot of boiling salted water until al dente. Drain in a colander and rinse under cold running water until cool. Drain well, shaking the colander to remove as much water as possible.

3. While the pasta is cooking, combine the sour cream, yogurt, dill, salt, and pepper in a bowl and whisk until blended. Add the pasta and toss until coated. Add the diced tomato and seafood and toss well. Let the salad stand at room temperature for about 30 minutes before serving. Check the seasoning before serving.

Barbecues and Other Main Events

While we've done our share of—and are not averse to—Park Avenue parties with champagne and caviar, most of our clients ask us to cater informal, low-budget occasions. From May through September we do enough outdoor barbecues to get a suntan without ever hitting the beach. When it's slack season, or if there's no backyard or deck, we're likely to do a buffet supper with braised or roasted meat or a stew as centerpiece.

In this chapter we've grouped the main events—poultry, meat, and fish dishes—that we've found work best for parties. Also included are some ideas for quick main courses that are suitable for family meals and small gatherings.

With most of the recipes, we've given serve-with suggestions, but as always we urge you to follow your own inclinations.

Blue Collar Barbecues

Being Blue Collar guys, we love a barbecue. We lug huge galvanized tubs to the site and fill them full of ice, beer, soda, and wine. For a big crowd, we set up six-foot charcoal grills and throw everything on them from handheld starters like ribs (page 43) or spiedini (page 39) to all-American hamburgers (plenty of ketchup and pickle relish on hand) to grilled trout, which we serve with papaya relish (page 143).

We build a fire with charcoal briquets as soon as we arrive, light them, and let them burn until the flames die down and the coals are gray. While the coals are burning down, we set out the chips and dips—we keep some Black Bean Dip (page 35) warm on the side of the grill—and pass around starters that we've prepared ahead and finished in the host's oven, like mini packets of Lone Star Shrimp (page 184).

The rest of the menu is built around dishes that can be served at room temperature like Black Bean Salad (page 218), Wild Rice and Broccoli Salad (page 225), and Roasted Asparagus (page 191). We always serve a big salad; we combine the greens (prewashed) and salad dressing only at the last minute when the bowl needs to be topped off.

It's amazing considering the amount of food and drink consumed when people eat out of doors—"it must be the country air" is the excuse often heard—but they still can handle dessert. We come prepared, usually with Blue Collar Brownies (page 252), Fresh Fruit Cobbler (page 234), Peach and Blueberry Pie (page 248).

Marinades

We always marinate meat or fish that's to be grilled, even hamburgers, with at least a veil of olive oil or a smear of grainy mustard or with one of the marinades listed below. These coatings serve both to flavor and to tenderize the food. Most of the marinades can be used interchangeably on chicken, pork, beef, or lamb. We use only delicate marinades for fish because we've found the more potent ones tend to overpower it. As always, though, we urge you to experiment and draw your own conclusions.

- Teriyaki Sauce (page 44)
- BCF 1-2-3 BBQ Sauce (page 45)
- Chili Rub (page 137)
- Mint Pesto (page 139)
- Honey Mustard Glaze (page 29)
- Dry herb marinade (page 134)
- Dill marinade for salmon (page 142)

Grilled Cornish hens are a favorite at barbecues. Guests get a whole bird each and have the pleasure of eating it with their bare hands. We partially cook the hens in the oven first. That way they're ready fast yet sure to be cooked through. With their honey-mustard coating, these are particularly good with Bread, Tomato, and Basil Salad (page 82) or at end-of-the-season cookouts with Butternut Squash Puree (page 204).

4 Cornish hens, 1 to 1¼ pounds each

Kosher salt

Freshly ground black pepper

⅓ cup grainy mustard

¼ cup honey

2 tablespoons white wine vinegar

2 teaspoons dried tarragon

1. Cut the backbones from the hens with a sturdy knife or pair of kitchen shears. Or ask the butcher to do this for you. Cut away any overhanging skin and fat. Rinse the hens inside and out and pat dry with paper towels. Sprinkle all sides of the hens generously with salt and pepper. Stir the mustard, honey, vinegar, and tarragon in a small bowl until blended. Use half of this mixture to coat all sides of the hens. Refrigerate the remaining marinade. Wrap the hens and refrigerate for 1 to 2 days.

2. Place the oven rack in the top position and heat the oven to 375°F.

3. Arrange the birds, skin side up, in a single layer in a roasting pan or baking dish large enough to hold them comfortably. Bake, rotating the pan once or twice, until the skin is light brown, about 40 minutes. *The hens may be prepared to this* point several hours in advance. Cool the hens to room temperature before refrigerating. Let the hens stand at room temperature 30 minutes before grilling.

4. Set up the grill, light the coals, and place the grill about 4 inches above. When the coals are ready, grill the hens, starting skin side up, until the skin is crisp and no trace of pink remains near the thickest part (like where the wing meets the breast) when poked with a knife, about 12 minutes. Serve hot.

Note: To cook the hens entirely in the oven, add about 15 minutes to the roasting time. Pour off the fat from the roasting pan halfway through cooking. Pass the hens under the broiler to crisp the skin.

Grilled Chicken Breasts

Makes 4 servings

These chicken breasts are too good to wait for grill time, so we broil them between sessions. Chris picked up the idea for dry marinades when he was working in the test kitchens of _Food & Wine_ magazine. Noted food writer Paula Wolfert came to demonstrate several duck recipes from Southwest France. One of them was a duck breast marinated with dried thyme, bay leaf, garlic, salt, and pepper. The result of this marinade made without liquid was an intense, "cured" flavor and a crisper texture. The lesson stuck, and we've been playing around with dry marinades ever since. Choose side dishes with mellow flavors, like Mashed Red Potatoes (page 199) or Fennel and Leek Gratin (page 194).

4 bone-in chicken breasts, with skin (about 2 pounds)

Kosher salt

Freshly ground black pepper

1½ teaspoons mixed dried herbs, such as oregano, rosemary, thyme, tarragon, basil, etc.

1 large clove garlic, finely chopped

1 lemon, cut into 4 wedges

_1._   Trim any overhanging fat from the chicken breasts. Sprinkle both sides of each breast generously with salt and pepper. Stir the dried herbs and the garlic together in a small bowl and press this mixture into all sides of the chicken breasts. Refrigerate for 1 to 2 days.

_2._   Remove the chicken breasts from the refrigerator 1 hour before grilling.

3. Set up the grill, light the coals, and place the grill 4 inches above them. When the coals are ready, broil the chicken, skin side down, until well browned, about 6 minutes. Turn the chicken skin side up and grill until the skin is deep golden brown and crisp and the chicken is cooked through with no trace of pink at the thickest part, about 8 minutes. Move the chicken pieces occasionally so they cook evenly. Serve hot with lemon wedges.

Grilled Pork Chops Teriyaki

Makes 4 servings

Salty, sweet, and spicy, teriyaki both flavors the meat and glazes it. Besides pork chops, you can use it on chicken breasts or tuna steaks. It scorches easily, so do thick pieces of meat like these chops over slow coals and move them to the side of the grill once they start to brown.

Four 1-inch-thick bone-in loin pork chops (about 2½ pounds)
½ cup Teriyaki Sauce (page 44)

1. Brush the chops generously with teriyaki sauce and marinate in the refrigerator for 30 to 60 minutes. Remove the chops to room temperature 30 minutes before grilling.

2. Set up the grill, light the coals, and place the grill about 4 inches from the heat. When the coals are ready, grill the chops until mahogany brown and the juice from the thickest part of the chop runs clear not pink when poked with a small knife, about 10 minutes per side. Move the chops on the grill as each side cooks to prevent overbrowning, but avoid turning the chops over more than once. Remove from the grill and brush with sauce. Let stand for 1 or 2 minutes before serving.

Grilled Chili-rubbed Flank Steak

Makes 6 servings

Flank steak is a very lean cut of beef that needs to be marinated to make it tender. You can use any one of several marinades, including Teriyaki Sauce (page 44) and Honey Mustard Glaze (page 29), but we like this chili treatment. Then we serve the steak with tortillas warmed on the grill, sour cream, Salsa Cruda (page 31), and Guacamole (page 34).

One 2-pound flank steak, well trimmed
Kosher salt
Freshly ground black pepper
1 to 2 tablespoons Chili Rub (recipe follows)
Lime wedges

1. Pat the flank steak thoroughly dry with paper towels. Sprinkle both sides of the steak with salt and pepper. Using your fingers, press the Chili Rub into both sides of the flank steak. Wrap the steak well and refrigerate for at least 4 hours or up to 2 days. The longer the steak marinates the more intense the flavor.

2. Remove the flank steak from the refrigerator 1 hour before grilling.

3. Set up the grill, light the coals, and place the grill 4 inches above them. When the coals are ready, place the flank steak on the grill and cook, turning once, until done, 12 to 15 minutes for rare, 15 to 20 minutes for medium. Let the meat rest for 5 minutes before slicing. Slice the flank against the grain (it's very easy to see) into thin strips, holding the knife at an angle to the cutting surface. Serve warm, accompanied by lime wedges.

Chili Rub

Makes about ¾ cup

From flank steak to fresh tuna, anything rubbed with this potent potion will benefit from a final drizzle of olive oil and shower of lime juice when it comes off the grill. Sprinkle the meat or fish with kosher salt and rub with about one tablespoon of the mix per pound. Let stand for at least four hours before grilling.

¼ cup chili powder

¼ cup oriental sesame oil or good quality olive oil

2 tablespoons fresh lime juice

2 tablespoons soy sauce

1 teaspoon minced garlic

Combine all the ingredients in a small bowl and stir until well blended. Transfer to a small lidded container and store in the refrigerator for up to 1 month.

Grilled Lamb Chops with Mint

Makes 4 servings

People who like lamb love grilled chops. They get a good crust while the meat stays tender and rare, something you just can't achieve under the home broiler. And there's no messy broiler clean-up either. We've suggested loin chops, but you could use rib chops or even baby rib chops as a handheld appetizer. Serve these with Roasted New Potatoes with Garlic (page 198) and a Watercress and Orange Salad with Roquefort (page 86). Don't forget the red wine.

8 thick loin lamb chops (about 2 pounds), trimmed of excess fat
Kosher salt
Freshly ground black pepper
½ cup Mint Pesto (recipe follows)
⅓ cup pine nuts or slivered almonds (optional)

1. Sprinkle the lamb chops with salt and pepper. Coat both sides of each chop with pesto, using about 1 tablespoon each. Set aside at room temperature until ready to grill, for up to 1 hour. Or the chops can be marinated and refrigerated for up to 1 day.

2. Set up the grill, light the coals, and place the grill 4 inches above them. When the coals are ready, grill the chops, turning once, until done, about 8 minutes for rare, 10 minutes for medium. Sprinkle with pine nuts or almonds, if desired, and serve immediately.

Mint Pesto

Makes about 1½ cups

Mint has an affinity for lamb, and this pesto is an obvious choice to slather on lamb chops or to stuff a boneless leg of lamb. (Take the pesto with you to the butcher and ask him to smear it on before rolling and tying the meat.) But the pesto is also good with chicken and shrimp, even steak. Allow about two tablespoons for every pound of meat.

4 cups (packed) fresh mint leaves

1 cup olive oil, preferably extra virgin

4 cloves garlic, roughly chopped

2 teaspoons sugar

¼ cup balsamic vinegar or red wine vinegar

Combine all the ingredients in a food processor or blender and process until smooth, 1 to 2 minutes. Transfer the pesto to a small container with a tight-fitting lid. *Pesto may be stored in the refrigerator for up to 1 month.*

A boned and butterflied leg of lamb provides a simple answer to the vexing question of how to feed a crowd at a barbecue. When you grill this cut, you turn only one piece of meat only one time (though you may want to cut it in two for easier handling). And because the meat is uneven, with thick and thin parts, you'll have both rare and well done slices, something for every taste. Marinate the meat with the dry rub suggested here or with Chili Rub (page 137).

One 7½-pound leg of lamb, butterflied (see Note)

3 tablespoons olive oil

4 cloves garlic, finely chopped

1 tablespoon kosher salt

2 teaspoons ground cumin

2 teaspoons ground coriander

½ teaspoon freshly ground black pepper

½ teaspoon crushed red pepper

4 bay leaves, torn or crumbled into small pieces

1. Open the lamb, fat side down, on a work surface. Cut out any small pieces of bone or gristle. Turn the lamb fat over and check again for bone or gristle. If necessary, trim the fat to a ¼-inch layer. (Don't remove all the fat; it will help flavor and moisten the meat during grilling.)

2. Combine the olive oil, garlic, salt, cumin, coriander, black pepper, red pepper, and bay leaves in a small bowl. Stir to a thick paste. Rub the paste evenly into all sides of the lamb. Fold the lamb in half, place it in a dish large enough to hold it comfortably, and cover tightly with plastic wrap. Refrigerate for 6 to 12 hours.

3. Remove the lamb from the refrigerator 1 hour before cooking. Set up the grill, light the coals, and place the grill about 4 inches from the heat. When the coals are ready, place the lamb, fat side up, on the grill and cook until the underside is seared, about 10 minutes. Move the lamb occasionally with a pair of tongs for even cooking, but don't flip it until the first side is cooked. Turn the lamb over and continue cooking for 10 to 15 minutes. At this point parts of the lamb should be medium rare, and other parts more well done. Check with an instant-reading thermometer: 130°F. for rare, 140°F. for medium. Remove the lamb to a cutting board and let it stand for about 5 minutes before carving. Carve the lamb on an angle into thin slices.

Notes: Though a simple enough task when you know what you're doing, butterflying a leg of lamb is best left to the butcher, who has the tools and technique for it. Order the lamb ahead of time.

The bay leaves sold in supermarkets come mostly from California or Turkey; they tend to be larger, sturdier, and stronger in flavor than others. If you are using these, reduce the amount listed by half. Look for small bay leaves from France, which is what we use when we're looking for a subtle bay flavor.

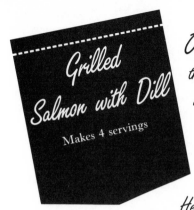

Grilled Salmon with Dill

Makes 4 servings

One of the best things about contemporary cooking in America is the "anything goes" feeling that has flowed from food writers and restaurant chefs into the backyards and kitchens of home cooks. Which is not to say the basic rules of cooking have changed—only how you bend them. While we both have classical training, neither of us feels limited by that.

Here Bill took the marinade for gravlax, the traditional Swedish dish of dry-cured salmon that is served raw, and applied it to salmon that's to be grilled. It's the perfect dish for a summer barbecue. Salmon marinated this way tends to cook a little faster than plain salmon, so be quick on the draw.

Four 6- to 7-ounce pieces of skinless salmon fillet, each about 1 to 1½ inches thick

1 tablespoon coarsely ground black pepper (see Note)

1 tablespoon chopped fresh dill

2 teaspoons sugar

1 teaspoon kosher salt

1. Pat the salmon dry with paper towels. Combine the pepper, dill, sugar, and salt in a small bowl and mix well. Rub the spice mixture evenly into all sides of the fillets. Refrigerate the fillets and marinate for 6 to 8 hours.

2. Set up the grill, light the coals, and place the grill 4 inches above them. When the coals are ready, brush the grill lightly with vegetable oil. Grill the salmon fillets, skin (flat) side down, about 4 inches from the heat until medium rare (still cool in the center), about 8 minutes, longer for more well done salmon. Turn them only once during cooking, using a long metal spatula. Transfer the salmon to serving plates and let stand for 1 or 2 minutes before serving.

Note: If you have a pepper mill that grinds peppercorns to a coarse consistency, use that. Otherwise, place some peppercorns on a work surface and slowly and carefully grind them with a flat heavy object, like the bottom of a small saucepan.

Grilled Trout with Papaya Relish

Makes 4 servings

The combination of fish and papaya strikes many people as odd, yet this dish was among the most popular on the menu when we worked together at a certain Manhattan restaurant. We updated the relish for our Blue Collar clientele and found its popularity undiminished. The dish goes well with a green salad tossed with an orange vinaigrette, such as the one for the watercress salad on page 86, or with fresh fennel, thinly sliced and tossed with lemon juice and olive oil.

Four 10-ounce trout, cleaned, or four 7-ounce salmon fillets

Olive oil

Kosher salt

Freshly ground black pepper

1 ripe papaya (see Note)

1 cucumber

1 teaspoon fresh lime juice

1½ teaspoons chopped fresh cilantro (optional)

1 small jalapeño, stemmed, seeded, and minced

2 tablespoons finely chopped red onion

¼ cup finely diced roasted red pepper

(continued)

1. Rub both sides of the fish with olive oil and sprinkle generously with salt and pepper.

2. Peel the papaya, cut it in half, and scoop out and reserve the seeds. Cut each half in half crosswise, and finely dice the pieces. Place the papaya in a small bowl. Peel the cucumber, cut it in half, scoop out and discard the seeds. Cut the flesh into pieces the same size as the papaya. Add the lime juice, cilantro, if using, jalapeño, onion, and red pepper and toss to mix. Season to taste with salt and pepper. *The fish and relish may be prepared to this point up to 6 hours in advance and refrigerated. Remove from the refrigerator 30 minutes before cooking.*

3. Set up the grill, light the coals, and place the grill about 4 inches from the coals. Lightly brush the grill with oil and grill the fish, turning only once, about 7 to 8 minutes for medium (with a cool center), 9 to 10 minutes for well done. Transfer the trout to serving plates and spoon a little relish over each piece. Sprinkle with some of the seeds, if desired. Pass the remaining relish separately.

Note: A ripe papaya is soft but not mushy, with colors ranging from yellow through rose to orange, with some green; a fruit with brown spots is acceptable. Harder fruit will ripen in 2 to 3 days at room temperature. The papaya should not see the inside of a refrigerator until dead ripe. Papaya seeds are edible.

Substitute diced fresh pineapple for the papaya.

When it comes to main courses, we like to turn the tables and give old cuts a new twist and new cuts an old twist. We treat turkey cutlets and ground turkey, which are low in price, like veal, which is not. We use these new cuts of turkey for piccata and for a loaf that is spicy and almost as smooth as a pâté. Our Veal and Artichoke Stew, on the other hand, has little in common with the bland blanquettes of bistro memory. Hunter's Chicken, City Style, made with mushrooms that grow in abandoned mines rather than under great oaks in primeval forests and with stewed tomatoes from a can, is but a distant relative of the classic *poulet sauté chasseur*.

Much of our repertoire is suited to the kind of casual parties we do a lot of. These dishes are crowd-pleasers, we're not ashamed to say. Most can be prepared ahead and reheated, making them practical for home entertaining as well.

In addition, we offer some suggestions for daily specials, which remain the greatest challenge for everyone, even foodies like us. Our Skillet Meals, for example, can be ready in thirty to forty-five minutes. Such dishes as Curry in a Hurry and Saffron Seafood Stew borrow a tried-and-true restaurant technique: A seasoned base is prepared ahead and refrigerated or frozen until needed. Then the dish can be finished in very short order, particularly if you choose to add cut-up boneless chicken breast or fish or shellfish, which cook quickly.

All of the cuts in this section are readily available in supermarkets. The only problem might be cutting up a chicken, but you can always ask the butcher or use a quartered chicken.

Turkey Piccata

Makes 4 servings

Chris's first job in a restaurant kitchen was in his New Jersey hometown at an Italian restaurant where the specialty was Northern Italian dishes. At that time, the hallmark of a Northern Italian restaurant was veal piccata, usually in a preparation that went heavy on the butter and wine. We've updated the dish, using turkey cutlets for economy and a minimum amount of butter. Serve this with Parmesan Polenta (page 228) and a big green salad.

Four 4-ounce turkey cutlets (see Note)

Kosher salt

Freshly ground black pepper

All-purpose flour

3 tablespoons unsalted butter

1 tablespoon vegetable oil

3 tablespoons dry white wine

¼ cup Chicken Broth, preferably homemade (page 53), or low-sodium canned broth

2 tablespoons finely chopped fresh parsley

1 tablespoons capers, rinsed and drained (optional)

1 tablespoon fresh lemon juice

1. Pat the cutlets dry with paper towels. Sprinkle both sides of each cutlet generously with salt and pepper. Coat both sides with flour, tapping off any excess flour. Place them on a dry surface. Measure out all the other ingredients and set them near the stove.

2. Heat 1 tablespoon of the butter and the oil in a large skillet over medium heat until the butter is bubbling. Add as many of the cutlet pieces as will fit

without overlapping. Sauté them until golden brown, about 3 minutes. Turn and repeat. Remove the cutlets to paper towels to drain. Repeat with the remaining cutlets.

3.   Pour off as much fat from the skillet as possible. Return the skillet to the heat and pour in the white wine. Let it boil until almost evaporated. Pour in the broth and boil until reduced by half. Add the parsley, capers, if using, lemon juice, and the remaining 2 tablespoons of butter. Boil until the butter is melted and incorporated into the sauce and the sauce is thick enough to lightly coat a spoon, about 2 minutes. Reduce the heat to very low. Return the cutlets to the skillet, turning to coat them evenly with sauce. Divide the turkey among serving plates, spooning extra sauce over each.

Note: Try to select four 4-ounce cutlets of the same thickness. If the cutlets aren't uniform, cut them as necessary to make 4 equal portions. If any of the cutlets are thicker than ¼ inch, pound them lightly between 2 sheets of plastic wrap with your hand or the bottom of a small saucepan until they are ¼ inch thick.

We used to think the most you could expect from ground turkey was ersatz hamburgers and meat loaf. Were we ever wrong! In one of our ongoing efforts to shave fat and calories from the menu, we started fooling around and came up with this incredible loaf. It's good warm but sensational cold, just the thing for a picnic or sandwiches. (We like it on pumpernickel.) Our secret ingredient is—are you ready for this?—corn flakes.

1 lemon

2 large eggs

2 tablespoons Dijon mustard

1 tablespoon Worcestershire sauce

2 tablespoons chopped fresh parsley

1 tablespoon chopped fresh tarragon or 2 teaspoons dried tarragon

1 teaspoon poultry seasoning

1 tablespoon kosher salt

1 teaspoon freshly ground black pepper

3 pounds ground turkey, preferably 10% fat

2 ribs celery, finely chopped

1 medium onion, finely chopped

⅔ cups dried breadcrumbs

⅔ cup crushed corn flakes (see Note)

⅓ cup ketchup or 2 tablespoons tomato paste mixed with 3 tablespoons warm water

1.   Set the oven rack in the center position and heat the oven to 375°F.

2. Scrub the lemon and remove the zest with a fine grater. Be sure to remove only the yellow part and not the bitter white pith. Squeeze the juice from the lemon. Combine the zest and juice, the eggs, mustard, Worcestershire, parsley, tarragon, poultry seasoning, salt, and pepper in a large bowl. Beat until well blended.

3. Crumble the ground turkey into the bowl and add the celery, onion, breadcrumbs, and corn flakes. Mix thoroughly with your hands, making sure all the ingredients are evenly distributed through the meat. Form the mixture into a 5 × 10-inch loaf in a 9 × 12-inch baking dish. Spread the ketchup evenly over the outside of the loaf.

4. Bake until the loaf is springy to the touch and juices from the center run clear not pink when poked with a fork, 45 minutes to 1 hour. Let stand for 5 to 10 minutes before cutting. Serve hot or cold. *May be refrigerated for up to 3 days.*

Note: You can use packaged corn flake crumbs, if you like, but we prefer to crush the cereal ourselves. You can do this in a food processor, pulsing several times for an uneven texture. For ⅔ cup crushed cornflakes, you will need about 2½ cups corn flakes.

Marie Styler's Chicken in Barber Paper

Makes 4 servings

For Marie Styler it was déjà vu all over again when she saw her son package a piece of chicken in parchment paper and bake it. When she was a little girl, her grandmother would send her to the barbershop for a piece of the coarse paper that was used to line the chairs. Sometimes she had to pay a few pennies, but more often than not, the barber would just give her the end of a roll. (Those were the gone-forever days when butchers gave away soup bones, too.) Her grandmother would wrap seasoned pieces of chicken in the paper and bake them. This is her recipe, as recollected by Chris's Mom. Serve it with Tomatoes Provençal (page 209) and Creamed Spinach (page 205).

One 3½-pound chicken, cut into 4 pieces (see Note)

Olive oil

Kosher salt

Freshly ground black pepper

1 cup dried breadcrumbs, either plain or seasoned

½ cup grated parmesan or romano

1 large onion, chopped

4 bay leaves

1. Trim any excess fat and skin from the chicken pieces. Brush all sides lightly with the olive oil and sprinkle them with salt and pepper. Mix the breadcrumbs and cheese in a bowl and coat the chicken pieces on all sides with this mixture.

2. Place a quarter of the chopped onion in the center of a 15 × 15-inch sheet of parchment paper or aluminum foil. Top with a bay leaf. Place 1 piece of chicken, skin side down, over the bay leaf. Bring 2 opposite ends of the paper to meet over the chicken. Crease them to seal in the chicken. Do the same with the 2 other ends to make a snug package for the chicken. Place the chicken package, seam side down, on a baking sheet. Repeat with the remaining chicken. Drizzle some olive oil over the packages. *The chicken can be prepared to this point up to 6 hours in advance. Bring the chicken to room temperature 30 minutes before baking.*

3. Set the oven rack in the uppermost position and heat the oven to 375°F.

4. Bake the chicken for about 45 minutes or until it is golden brown. Open a package to check. Serve immediately.

Note: Have the butcher remove the backbone and wing tips of a whole chicken and cut it into 2 breast/wing and 2 leg/thigh pieces. Or use a quartered chicken (wing tips removed).

We find roaster chicken breasts to have more taste and better texture than the ubiquitous boneless and skinless ones. Here we take slices and make "sandwiches" with prosciutto, basil, and parmesan. It's a high flavor–low effort dish. Serve it hot with White Beans and Kale (page 216) or cold with a mixed green salad. Prosciutto is the key element in this dish, so don't stint.

Olive oil or vegetable oil

1 boneless and skinless roaster chicken breast (about 2 pounds), cut into 8 thin slices (see Note)

Freshly ground black pepper

¼ pound thinly sliced prosciutto (about 12 slices)

12 to 15 large basil leaves, rinsed and dried

1 tablespoon grated parmesan

1 egg, well beaten

2 tablespoons dried breadcrumbs

1.   Heat the oven to 350°F. Lightly oil a 9 × 13-inch baking dish.

2.   Make 4 pairs of equal-sized chicken slices and lay the pairs side by side on your work surface. Sprinkle the chicken with pepper. Cover one of each pair of slices with prosciutto, making an even layer and extending it all the way to the edge of the chicken slice. Do the same with the basil. Sprinkle the other half of the pair with parmesan and place it, cheese side down, over the basil, forming a neat package. Brush the tops with beaten egg then sprinkle them with breadcrumbs. Transfer the chicken to the prepared baking dish. *The chicken may be prepared to this point for up to 1 day in advance. Cover and refrigerate. Let the chicken stand at room temperature for 30 minutes before baking.*

3.　Bake the chicken until the breadcrumbs are golden brown and the chicken is cooked through, about 25 minutes. Serve hot.

Note:　Many of the big-name chicken producers sell presliced roaster breasts. Check your market for these and count the slices before buying. If not available, slice the breasts yourself or ask your butcher to do it.

Roasted Chicken with Soy-Honey Glaze

Makes 6 servings

We like to marinate a whole chicken overnight in this sweet-and-sour concoction. The roasted bird turns a rich mahogany color and is full of flavor. The sauce takes a little longer than usual to finish, but it's well worth the extra time that goes into it. Serve this with Coconut Rice (page 222) or Roasted Asparagus (page 191).

One 6- to 8-pound roasting chicken
1 cup orange juice
¼ cup honey
2 tablespoons soy sauce
¼ teaspoon freshly ground black pepper
3 ribs celery, finely chopped
1 navel orange, scrubbed and cut into 8 wedges
1 tablespoon cornstarch
¾ cup boiling water

1.　Pull the excess fat from the cavity and neck of the chicken. Wash the chicken inside and out and blot dry with paper towels. Combine the orange juice, honey, soy sauce, and pepper in a bowl large enough to hold the chicken and stir until the honey is dissolved. Add the celery and orange and place the chicken in the bowl, turning it to coat all sides. Cover and refrigerate the chicken for at least 12 hours, turning it once or twice in the marinade.

2.　Remove the chicken and let stand at room temperature for one hour before cooking.

3.　Heat the oven to 350°F.

4.　Remove the chicken from the marinade and place it in a roasting pan, preferably on a roasting rack. Strain the marinade into a small bowl and place the celery and orange in the cavity of the chicken. Roast the chicken until done, about 1½ hours. Check by poking the thickest parts, such as where the leg meets the backbone or the wing meets the breast, with a skewer or a small knife—the juices should run clear not pink. Baste the chicken occasionally during roasting using about half of the strained marinade. The skin should be very well browned.

5. Remove the chicken to a cutting board or serving platter. Scoop out and discard the orange and celery from the cavity. Let the chicken rest for 10 minutes.

6. Pour the remaining marinade into a skillet and stir in the cornstarch until it is dissolved. Tilt the roasting pan and spoon or pour off the fat. Add the boiling water to the pan and scrape up as much of the browned bits as you can. Pour this mixture into the skillet with the marinade and bring to a boil over medium heat. Boil the sauce, stirring occasionally, until reduced to a consistency you like. You may prefer to serve more of a thinner, mildly flavored sauce, or less of a thicker, more concentrated sauce. Keep the sauce warm over low heat while you carve or cut the chicken. Spoon some of the sauce over the chicken and pass the rest separately.

When you cut up a chicken before roasting it rather than after, the marinade penetrates the meat more deeply. The skin is also crispier, and there is less fat. While this chicken is quite wonderful hot, we find it's even better served at room temperature. It's especially nice with Signor Mario's Baked Cauliflower (page 192) and a big green salad.

One 3½-pound chicken, cut into 6 pieces (see Note)

1 lemon, thinly sliced

2 tablespoons olive oil

1 teaspoon dried rosemary

1 teaspoon kosher salt

Large pinch freshly ground black pepper

1. Toss the chicken pieces in a large bowl with the remaining ingredients until the pieces are evenly coated. Transfer the chicken, scraping the sides of the bowl to remove all the marinade, to a storage container. Cover the container tightly and refrigerate the chicken for at least 4 hours or up to 2 days. The longer the chicken marinates, the deeper the flavors of the marinade will penetrate the chicken.

2. Remove the chicken from the refrigerator about 30 minutes before roasting.

3. Heat the oven to 425°F. Line a heavy baking pan with aluminum foil.

4. Arrange the chicken pieces in a single layer, skin side up, in the pan. Roast the chicken until the skin is golden brown and crisp and the chicken is very tender, about 40 minutes. No trace of pink should remain near the bone. Poke the thickest part of the chicken, like the center of the thigh, for example, with a small sharp knife. The juices should run clear.

Note: Ask your butcher to remove the backbone and wing tips and cut the chicken into breast/wing, leg, and thigh pieces. Or buy a chicken already cut into quarters. Cut the leg in two at the joint and remove the wing tips and any overhanging skin before marinating.

Arroz con Pollo, Gringo Style

Makes 4 servings

Long slow cooking makes peppers almost melt. The more colors and types you use—even a few chiles—the better the dish. This one-pot meal is great for informal parties, like covered-dish or potluck suppers. Serve it with Blue Collar Black Bean Salad (page 218) or a BCF Caesar Salad (page 80), tossed with cherry tomatoes, depending on the season.

1 tablespoon olive oil

One 3½-pound chicken, backbone removed, cut into 8 pieces
   (page 165)

2 cups pepper strips, from about 3 large bell peppers or any mix of
   green, yellow, or red bell peppers and chiles

3 scallions, chopped

1 clove garlic, thinly sliced

1½ cups water

1 cup converted rice

1 tablespoon chopped fresh cilantro

1 teaspoon salt

Pinch freshly ground black pepper

1. Heat the oil in a large ovenproof skillet or Dutch oven over medium heat. Add as many of the chicken pieces as will fit in a single layer. Cook the chicken, turning the pieces as necessary, until well browned on all sides, about 10 minutes. Repeat, if necessary, with the remaining chicken pieces. Remove the chicken to drain on paper towels.

2. Drain or spoon off almost all the oil from the skillet. Add the peppers, scallions, and garlic. Sauté, stirring occasionally, until softened and browned, about 4 minutes. Spread the peppers into an even layer over the bottom of the skillet and top with the chicken pieces. Add the water, rice, cilantro, salt, and pepper and bring to a boil.

3. Reduce the heat to very low, cover the skillet, and cook until the rice is tender and the chicken is cooked through, about 50 minutes. If there is a little liquid left, it will be absorbed by the rice. Transfer the chicken and rice to a serving platter or place directly on serving plates.

Note: You may cook this dish in the oven. Prepare the recipe through Step 2 in a large skillet and transfer the contents to a 9 × 13-inch baking dish. Cover the dish with aluminum foil and bake in a 350°F. oven until the rice is tender and the chicken is cooked, about 50 minutes.

Curry in a Hurry

Makes 6 servings

We pinched this name from a funky pink and purple Indian cafeteria we used to frequent on Lexington Avenue in New York's Little India. We make a curry sauce or "base"—a seasoned liquid in restaurant lingo—ahead of time and finish the dish at the last minute. Bases like this and the one for Saffron Seafood Stew (page 186) are a lifesaver in a busy restaurant kitchen; they can be at home too. Serve the curry with steamed white or brown rice and an array of condiments—chutney, yogurt, raisins, toasted peanuts, toasted coconut, wedges of lime—as many or as few as you want. Salsa Cruda (page 31) is also good.

¼ cup peanut or vegetable oil

2 small white onions, finely chopped

3 cloves garlic, sliced

1 tablespoon mild to hot curry powder, preferably Madras

2 cups Chicken Broth, preferably homemade (page 53), or low-sodium canned broth

½ cup unsweetened coconut milk (see Note)

¼ cup fresh lime juice

One 3½-pound chicken, backbone removed, cut into 8 pieces (page 165), or 1½ to 2 pounds boneless and skinless chicken cutlets, cut into 2-inch dice

1. Heat 2 tablespoons of the oil in a saucepan over medium heat. Add the onions and garlic, reduce the heat to low, and cook, stirring occasionally, until the onions are golden brown, about 8 minutes. Add the curry powder and cook, stirring, for 1 to 2 minutes. Add the broth and coconut milk and bring to a boil. Reduce the heat and simmer, uncovered, for 20 minutes. Cool to room temperature. Puree the mixture in a food processor or in batches in a blender. Stir in ¼ cup of the lime juice. *The curry sauce can be made up to 3 days in advance and refrigerated.*

2. Heat the remaining oil in a large skillet over medium heat. Add the chicken and sauté, turning as necessary, until lightly browned, about 12 minutes. Add just enough of the curry sauce to generously coat the chicken and bring to a boil. Reduce the heat, and simmer, uncovered, until the chicken pieces on the bone are tender, about 30 minutes or the diced chicken cutlets are cooked through, about 8 minutes. Check the seasoning, adding salt, pepper, or lime juice if needed.

Note: Canned unsweetened coconut milk is available in Asian grocery stores and some specialty markets. You can also make your own. Combine ¾ cup of water and ½ cup shredded coconut, preferably unsweetened, in a blender jar. Blend until the coconut is very finely chopped. Pour the mixture into a fine sieve and press to extract as much of the liquid as possible. If you used sweetened coconut to make the coconut milk, start with less than the amount called for in the curry sauce, taste, and add more if desired.

Variations

Shrimp Curry: Substitute 2 pounds large (21 to 25 per pound) shrimp, peeled and deveined (page 41), for the chicken in Step 2. Sauté the shrimp just until they start to turn pink. Add the curry sauce and simmer, uncovered, until the shrimp are cooked through, about 2 minutes.

Vegetable Curry: Substitute 6 cups mixed cut-up vegetables, such as onions, mushrooms, broccoli, cauliflower, zucchini, peas, cooked potatoes, etc. (no hard vegetables like carrots or parsnips, though) for the chicken in Step 2. Sauté until lightly browned, add the curry sauce, and simmer, uncovered, until cooked through, about 8 minutes for bite-size pieces.

Skillet Meals

Although we appreciate long-simmered stews and braised meats as much as the next guy (in fact, we've included several recipes for them), we remain dedicated to finding new ways to put a good meal on the table fast, day in and day out. What we call skillet meals is one of those ways.

The idea is to put ingredients together in a skillet and let them cook without further ado until it's time to finish the dish. The whole operation takes more or less half an hour, with about five minutes attention at the beginning and again at the end. You can even prepare the dish partly or entirely in advance and reheat it quickly when you're ready to eat.

Skillet meals require a main ingredient that is both tender and flavorful, like chicken on the bone (rather than cutlets) as on page 164 or pork medallions (page 166). The liquid used to deglaze the pan has to do double duty, adding flavor as well as making a sauce. Obviously, the main ingredient, seasoning, and liquid should be compatible.

Following is a basic outline for making a skillet meal. Fill in the blanks with your choice of ingredients. To work at near-professional speed, measure out the ingredients and line up the equipment first.

Seasoning the food. Season the (meat) with (pepper and salt, a dry marinade [page 134], or mustard).

Coating with flour. Toss the meat in flour and shake or tap off the excess. The flour helps seal in juices and also thickens the sauce.

Browning the food. Brown the meat in hot oil, without crowding the pan. Remove the meat and brown (vegetables) such as onions and garlic and/or mushrooms. Keep the heat high enough to maintain a lively sizzle but not so high that the food sticks or burns. Browning seals in juices, adds color, and enriches the flavor of the dish.

Deglazing the pan. Pour or spoon off the fat, and add (liquid). This could be wine and water, broth, tomato sauce, even canned stewed tomatoes. Bring the liquid to a boil and scrape up the bits that stuck to the bottom of the pan. Add (additional flavorings)—herbs, spices, hot peppers—at this point.

Simmering the dish. Return the food to the pan, cover, and adjust the heat. Simmer until done. Check and adjust the seasoning about halfway through and again just before serving.

This is the Blue Collar version of the classic French dish poulet sauté chasseur (Chicken, Hunter Style), in which chicken is cooked with mushrooms, wine, and tomato sauce flavored with tarragon. As urban foragers, we've found canned stewed tomatoes, which we use in this recipe and many others, to be an invaluable discovery. While you could serve the dish with buttered noodles or boiled potatoes, we prefer our own Mashed Red Potatoes (page 199).

One 3- to 3½-pound chicken, backbone removed, cut into 8 pieces (see Note)

Kosher salt

Freshly ground black pepper

¾ cup all-purpose flour

½ cup vegetable oil

1 tablespoon unsalted butter

1 medium onion, cut in half and thinly sliced

½ pound mushrooms, wiped cleaned and thinly sliced

1 clove garlic, thinly sliced

½ cup red wine

One 14½-ounce can stewed tomatoes

½ cup water

1½ teaspoons dried tarragon

1. Remove the skin from the chicken pieces if you like. Pat the chicken pieces dry with paper towels and sprinkle them generously with salt and pepper. Place the chicken pieces into a bowl, pour the flour on top, and turn the chicken until well coated on all sides. Heat the oil in a large skillet over medium heat. Shake the excess flour from each piece of chicken and slide it away from you into the hot oil. Put only as many pieces of chicken in the skillet as will fit without touching; overcrowding lowers the temperature of the oil and makes it difficult to brown the chicken. Cook the chicken over medium heat until golden, about 2 to 3 minutes on each side. Reduce the heat slightly if the chicken starts to spatter. Remove the chicken pieces to paper towels to drain. Repeat, if necessary, with the remaining chicken pieces.

2. Pour off the oil and return the skillet to the heat. Add the butter. When it has melted, add the onion, mushrooms, and garlic. Cook, stirring, until lightly browned, 1 to 2 minutes. Slowly pour in the red wine, scraping the bottom of the skillet, and cook until reduced by half. Add the tomatoes, water, tarragon, ½ teaspoon salt, and ¼ teaspoon pepper. Bring to a boil. Return the chicken pieces to the skillet and mix well to coat with sauce. Cover the skillet and reduce the heat until the liquid is barely simmering. Cook until the chicken is tender, about 35 to 45 minutes, stirring every 10 to 15 minutes. Adjust the seasoning if necessary. *The chicken may be prepared entirely up to 1 day in advance. Cool to room temperature before refrigerating. Reheat over low heat, adding a small amount of water if necessary to restore the sauce to its original consistency.* Serve hot.

Note: Ask your butcher or meat man to cut a whole chicken into 8 serving pieces for you. If that's not possible, buy a quartered chicken, cut each leg into 2 pieces at the joint, and cut the breast/wing pieces into 2 roughly equal pieces right through the thin breast bones. Cut away the wing tips and trim any excess fat from the chicken.

Pork Medallions with Hot Cherry Peppers

Makes 4 servings

We often open the refrigerator and look on the door instead of the shelves for inspiration. Such condiments as mustard, mayo, and ketchup; olives, capers, and anchovy paste; pestos and marinades—all these and much more get tucked into those narrow shelves. A jar of hot cherry peppers is always on our fridge door. We use them to spark pasta dishes, marinades for chicken, hamburgers, and skillet dinners like this one.

1 medium onion

Four 5- to 6-ounce pork medallions, cut from the rib end and trimmed of all fat

Kosher salt

Freshly ground black pepper

All-purpose flour

2 tablespoons olive oil or vegetable oil, or as needed

3 cloves garlic, thinly sliced

⅓ cup dry red wine

⅔ cup Chicken Broth, preferably homemade (page 53), or low-sodium canned broth

¼ cup sliced hot cherry peppers (See Note)

1. Peel the onion, cut it in half through the core and then crosswise into thin slices. Pat the pork dry with paper towels and generously sprinkle both sides of each piece with salt and pepper. Coat the medallions in flour, tapping off any excess.

2. Heat two tablespoons of the oil in a large heavy skillet over medium heat. Check the oil by sprinkling a little flour over the surface. When the oil is hot enough, the flour will sizzle. Carefully place the medallions in the skillet. Cook until the underside is well browned, about 3 minutes. Move the pieces with tongs occasionally so they brown evenly. Turn the pieces and cook until the second side is browned, about 3 minutes. Remove the medallions to paper towels to drain.

3. Carefully pour off all but a thin layer of fat from the skillet. Or if the medallions have absorbed all the oil, pour in a small amount. Reduce the heat to low, add the onions and garlic, and cook, stirring occasionally, until the onions are a deep golden brown, about 10 minutes.

4. Increase the heat to high, add the wine, and cook until only about 1 tablespoon remains. Add the broth and peppers. Bring to a boil and boil for 1 minute. Return the medallions to the skillet. Cook, turning the medallions once or twice, until no trace of pink remains in the center and the pan juices are thick enough to coat a spoon, about 4 minutes. Transfer the medallions to serving plates, spooning some the sauce and onions over each piece. Serve hot.

Note: Cherry peppers packed in vinegar are available in many supermarkets and Italian delicatessens and specialty shops. If you can't find cherry peppers, use hot pepper rings or pickled jalapeños. Remove the stems and cut the peppers into ¼-inch strips before measuring. Leave the seeds in for a spicier dish; scrape them out for a mellower effect. Wash your hands after handling the cherry peppers and avoid touching your eyes.

Roasted Picnic Ham with Sauerkraut

Makes 6 servings

When Blue Collar Food plans an informal winter party, we think hearty. We like the kind of food that braces you for piercing winds and swirling snowflakes. This dish has its origins in those Central European roast pork dishes that have dumplings or——as in this case——potatoes roasted in the pan with sauerkraut. Since the modern American pig has been bred to be slim, the loin is too lean and dry for this treatment. The shoulder or picnic ham, a bone-in roast with a thick layer of fat under the skin, however, is perfect. Long slow roasting renders most of the fat and leaves crispy cracklings to mix in with the kraut. The cut doesn't carve out into neat slices, but so what! This is not a dish to eat by candlelight.

One 6-pound picnic ham

2 tablespoons peanut or vegetable oil

1 teaspoon kosher salt

½ teaspoon freshly ground black pepper

2 pounds small new potatoes, scrubbed and cut in half

4 small onions, cut into quarters through the core

One 2-pound bag of sauerkraut, rinsed briefly and drained

1. Heat the oven to 400°F.

2. Lightly score the fat side of the ham at 1-inch intervals. Rub the ham with the oil, salt, and pepper. Place the ham in the center of a large shallow roasting pan.

3. Roast the ham for 15 minutes. Scatter the potatoes and onions around it and reduce the heat to 350°F. Roast for 1 hour.

4.　Stir the sauerkraut into the potatoes and onions until evenly distributed. Roast for 30 minutes, or until an instant-reading thermometer inserted into the thickest part of the ham registers 145° to 150°F. Remove the ham to a cutting board and let it stand for 10 minutes before carving. Turn off the oven and return the vegetables to the oven to keep warm. If you like, trim the excess fat from the ham before carving. Cut the ham into thin slices more or less parallel to the bone. Serve some of the sauerkraut mixture with each portion of ham.

Note:　An instant-reading thermometer is a good kitchen tool. It's ideal for testing large roasts like this one or the lamb on page 140 and for taking the temperature of yogurt, custard, water for yeast, and the like. The thermometer costs just a couple of bucks and will save you years of pork and pudding angst.

Somewhere early in the evolution of the meatball, it probably tasted like this. In Italy, meatballs are usually made with more than one kind of meat and often seasoned with a sweet spice like nutmeg. The spinach is our addition; it adds a note of freshness. If you make the meatballs in tomato sauce, serve them with Blue Collar's Spaghetti with Fried Garlic (page 100); if you use broth, serve them with buttered noodles or Brown Rice Pilaf (page 224). Mini-meatballs made with about a rounded tablespoon of the meat mixture make good cocktail party fare.

1 pound lean ground pork

1 pound lean ground beef

One 10-ounce box frozen chopped spinach, defrosted and drained

2 eggs, beaten well

2 tablespoons dried breadcrumbs

¼ cup grated parmesan or romano

1 small clove garlic, finely chopped

1½ tablespoons kosher salt

¼ teaspoon freshly ground black pepper

Pinch grated nutmeg

⅓ cup vegetable oil

All-purpose flour

2 cups Tomato Sauce, preferably homemade (page 95), Chicken Broth (page 53), beef broth, preferably homemade, or water

1. Crumble the ground pork and beef into a large bowl. Beat the spinach, eggs, breadcrumbs, cheese, garlic, salt, pepper, and nutmeg in a small bowl until blended. Add the egg mixture to the meat and mix well with your hands until completely incorporated. Form the mixture into 12 equal-size meatballs and set aside.

2. Heat the oil in a large skillet over medium heat. While the oil is heating, roll the meatballs in flour until well coated. Shake the excess flour from the meatballs and carefully place them in the skillet as you go. Brown the meatballs, turning them as necessary, on all sides, about 5 minutes. Remove them to paper towels to drain as they are done. Work in batches if necessary to prevent overcrowding the skillet.

3. When the meatballs are browned, pour off all the fat from the skillet. Add the Tomato Sauce and bring to a boil. Return the meatballs to the skillet, cover, and reduce the heat to a bare simmer. Cook until the meatballs are firm and the sauce is thick, about 50 minutes. Check the seasoning of the sauce, adjust if necessary, and serve the meatballs directly from the skillet. *The meatballs may be made entirely in advance and refrigerated for 2 days. They may be frozen for up to 2 months.*

Note: If you are using broth or water instead of Tomato Sauce, you may find it necessary to thicken the sauce. To do this, before returning the meatballs to the skillet, bring the sauce to a boil and boil until it is reduced enough to lightly coat a spoon. Or mix 1 tablespoon sour cream with 1 teaspoon all-purpose flour and whisk this mixture into the sauce after removing the skillet from the heat.

Joan's Pot Roast

Makes 6 servings

Joan Kilbride, aka Bill's mother-in-law, says she "used to be one hell of a cook." As far as we're concerned, she still is. This pot roast, with ingredients like dried onion-herb mix, instant beef broth, and Cherry Heering, may have a retro feel, but there's nothing dated about its flavor.

One 2½-pound piece eye round
Kosher salt
Freshly ground black pepper
All-purpose flour
3 tablespoons American-style mustard, such as French's or Gulden's
4 tablespoons (½ stick) margarine
5 cups water
½ cup sweet brandy, such as Cherry Heering (optional)
1 2-ounce package Lipton Recipe Secrets Onion
2 packets MBT beef broth (see Note)
1 bay leaf
5 carrots, peeled and cut into 2-inch pieces
4 to 5 new potatoes, scrubbed and cut into quarters
1 large onion, cut into large pieces

1. Pat the meat dry with paper towels and sprinkle all sides with salt and pepper. Roll the meat in flour to coat and tap off excess flour. Spread all sides with a thin even coating of mustard.

2. Heat the margarine in a heavy 4- to 5-quart pot with a tight-fitting lid over medium heat. When the margarine is melted and bubbling, carefully add the meat. Brown the meat, turning it with tongs to brown all sides evenly, about 10 minutes. Pour the water and brandy, if using, into the pot. Scrape up any bits stuck to the bottom. Add the soup mix, beef broth packets, and bay leaf. Reduce the heat to low, cover the pot, and cook for 1½ hours. Turn the meat every 15 to 20 minutes and check that the liquid remains at a bare simmer.

3. Remove the lid and add the carrots, potatoes, and onion. Cook, uncovered, at a low simmer until the meat is tender, 1 to 1½ hours. Turn the meat every 15 to 20 minutes.

4. Transfer the meat to a carving board and let stand for at least 10 minutes. Check the sauce. If you would like it a little thicker, increase the heat to high and boil until it is slightly thickened. Thinly slice the meat. Serve some meat and vegetables with a little of the sauce and pass the remaining sauce separately.

Note: If MBT is not available, substitute 1 teaspoon cornstarch dissolved in some cold water and 2 beef bouillon cubes.

Blue Collar Beef Stew

Makes 6 servings

This recipe outlines the basic procedure for making stew: Brown meat and vegetables, add liquid, and simmer until tender. We suggest you use it as a guide, changing the meat, vegetables, and liquid to suit your fancy. You can also customize this recipe by adding a dollop of grainy mustard with the liquid, or of sour cream at the end, or seasoning the stew with mixed chopped herbs. Be our guest.

One 14-ounce package soup vegetables (see Note)

1½ pounds lean chuck or bottom round

1 tablespoon kosher salt

½ teaspoon freshly ground black pepper

¼ cup all-purpose flour

¼ cup peanut oil

½ cup dry red wine

3 cups water

4 small red new potatoes, scrubbed and quartered

1. Prepare the soup vegetables: Peel and trim the parsnips, carrots, turnips, and onions; trim the celery. Cut all vegetables into large dice.

2. Trim the meat of fat and gristle. Cut into 1-inch cubes. Pat the meat dry, place it in a medium bowl, and toss with the salt and pepper. Sprinkle the flour over the meat and toss until the meat is evenly coated.

3. Heat the oil in a wide heavy pot over medium-high heat. Brown the meat in batches, adding only as much meat to the pot as will fit without touching. Cook, turning the meat, until evenly and well browned on all sides, about 7 minutes. Remove the meat to drain on paper towels and repeat with the remaining pieces if necessary. Adjust the heat to maintain a lively sizzle without smoking or burning. Brown the vegetables.

4.   Add the wine and water, scraping up any bits from the bottom, and bring to a boil. Return the meat to the pot and adjust the heat to simmering. Simmer, uncovered, for 30 minutes, stirring occasionally.

5.   Add the potatoes, partly cover the pot, and simmer until the potatoes and meat are tender, about 1 hour. Skim the fat from the surface occasionally. Check the seasoning, adjust as necessary, and serve hot.

Note: Many supermarkets sell packages of soup vegetables, which usually contain 1 or 2 small turnips, carrots, parsnips, small onions, and ribs of celery. If such a package is not available, use 1 medium white turnip, 2 medium carrots, 2 medium parsnips, 2 small onions, and 2 ribs celery.

Veal and Artichoke Stew

Makes 4 servings

Frozen artichokes are terrific to keep on hand for everything from pizza to grilled vegetable skewers to this stew, which has become a favorite on our fall and winter catering menus. Prepared at home, it makes an elegant entrée for a dinner party. Serve the stew with buttered noodles or new potatoes.

1½ pounds boneless veal neck or shoulder

2 teaspoons kosher salt

½ teaspoon freshly ground black pepper

¼ cup all-purpose flour

¼ cup vegetable oil

2 cups sliced button mushrooms (about ¾ pound)

1 medium onion, thinly sliced

2 tablespoons balsamic vinegar

3 cups water

One 9-ounce box frozen artichokes, defrosted and drained

1 teaspoon dried tarragon or Italian seasoning or Dijon mustard

½ cup heavy cream or ½ cup sour cream beaten with 1 tablespoon all-purpose flour

2 tablespoons finely chopped fresh parsley

1. Cut the veal into 1-inch cubes and trim any fat or gristle if necessary. Toss the veal in a bowl with the salt and pepper until the veal is evenly seasoned. Add the flour and toss until the veal is evenly coated.

2. Heat the oil in a large heavy sauté pan over medium heat. Add half the veal. Cook, stirring occasionally and adjusting the heat so there is always a lively sizzle, until the veal is deep golden brown on all sides, about 8 minutes, possibly longer if the veal is giving off a lot of liquid. Remove the veal to paper towels to drain and repeat with the remaining veal. Pour off almost all of the fat from the pan and add the mushrooms and onion. Sauté, stirring occasionally, until the onion is golden brown, about 4 minutes. Pour the vinegar into 2 cups of the water and add to the pan, stirring to scrape up the bits stuck to the bottom. Add the artichokes and tarragon. Return the meat to the pan. Reduce the heat, cover, and simmer, stirring once or twice and adding more water as necessary, until the meat is done, about 45 minutes to 1 hour.

3. Transfer the veal to a serving dish with a slotted spoon. Increase the heat to high, stir in the cream or sour cream–flour mixture, and boil until the sauce is thickened to your liking. Check the seasoning and pour the sauce over the veal and vegetables. Sprinkle the parsley on top and serve. *The stew may be prepared entirely in advance up to the addition of the cream and refrigerated for up to 3 days. Reheat the veal before adding the cream and proceed as in step 3 to finish the dish.*

Variation

Substitute 1½ pounds shoulder of lamb cut into 1-inch cubes and trimmed of fat for the veal. It will take about the same amount of time to cook. Skim the stew before serving. Omit the cream at the end.

Lamb shanks meet Blue Collar criteria—they're a cheap cut, but they don't shortchange you on flavor. We braise them with an eclectic mix of Mediterranean ingredients—coffee, cumin, and coriander from the Middle East, olives and oranges from Sicily. The result is a rich and mellow dish, which benefits from standing for a day before serving. This recipe is for two.

To make it for a crowd, use cut-up shanks. Serve the dish with Golden Couscous (page 230) or Brown Rice Pilaf (page 224).

1 teaspoon kosher salt

½ teaspoon ground cumin

½ teaspoon ground coriander

Large pinch freshly ground black pepper

2 lamb shanks (see Note)

1 orange

2 tablespoons peanut oil or vegetable oil

2 ribs celery, finely diced

1 carrot, peeled and finely diced

1 medium onion, finely diced

2 cloves garlic, peeled and thinly sliced

1 cup very strong brewed coffee or espresso

One 8-ounce can stewed tomatoes

¼ cup coarsely chopped pitted green olives (about ⅓ cup before
    pitting)

1. Combine the salt, cumin, coriander, and pepper in a small bowl and mix well. Pat the shanks dry and rub the spice mixture into the meaty part of the shanks. The shanks can be cooked right away or refrigerated for up to 1 day.

2. Scrub the orange and using a vegetable peeler remove the colored zest, leaving the white pith behind. Cut the orange in half and squeeze the juice.

3. Heat the oil over medium heat in a deep pot large enough to hold the shanks. Add the shanks and cook them, turning as necessary, until they are well browned on all sides, about 10 minutes. Adjust the heat so there is a lively sizzle without the oil smoking. Remove the shanks and carefully pour off about half the fat in the pot. Add the celery, carrot, onion, and garlic and cook, stirring often, until the vegetables are wilted and browned, about 6 minutes. Return the shanks to the pot and add the orange juice and zest, the coffee, tomatoes, and olives. Pour in enough water to come halfway up the shanks and bring to a boil. Reduce the heat to a simmer, cover the pot, and braise the shanks until tender in the thickest part, about 1 hour. Turn the shanks every 20 minutes or so.

4. Remove from the heat. Remove the shanks from the pot. Let the liquid stand for 1 or 2 minutes and skim any fat from the surface. Bring the sauce to a boil and boil until the liquid is reduced by about half and is thick enough to lightly coat a spoon. Return the shanks to the sauce and heat through. Serve hot, spooning some of the sauce over each serving.

Note: If you are cooking 2 or 4 shanks, ask the butcher to trim the shank bone even with the meat so they fit more easily in the pot. (Throw in the bone ends for more flavor.) For a crowd, ask him to saw the shanks into two-inch pieces.

Bill picked up this recipe when he was the chef at Caffe Bondi, a Sicilian restaurant in New York's Flatiron district. It's almost shamefully simple, but remember the simpler the dish the more essential it is that the ingredients be top rate—the freshest of fish, homemade tomato sauce, and garden fresh herbs if possible. For a Sicilian feast, serve Signor Mario's Baked Cauliflower (page 192) and Roasted Asparagus (page 191).

1 pound flounder, sole, or other flatfish fillets

Olive or vegetable oil

Kosher salt

Freshly ground black pepper

1 tablespoon dry white wine (optional)

½ cup Tomato Sauce, preferably homemade (page 95)

1 to 2 teaspoons finely chopped fresh herbs, such as thyme, rosemary, sage, basil, or any combination

1 lemon, cut in half

1. If the fish fillets are very thin (more than 4 to a pound), fold them in half crosswise. If they are very thick (2 to 4 to a pound), cut them in half lengthwise along the center crease. Choose a baking dish that the fillets will fit into in a single layer and coat it lightly with oil. Arrange the fillets in the dish and sprinkle them lightly with salt and pepper. Stir the wine, if using, into the Tomato Sauce and spoon the sauce over the fillets. Sprinkle the herbs over the top. Cover the dish tightly with aluminum foil. *The fillets may be prepared to this point up to 1 day in advance and refrigerated. Remove from the refrigerator 30 minutes before baking.*

2. Heat the oven to 375°F.

3. Bake the fillets, covered, until the juices in the dish are bubbling and the fillets are just cooked through, about 12 minutes. Squeeze a little lemon juice over the fillets and serve hot, passing the cut lemon separately.

Sautéed Fillet of Cod with Savoy Cabbage

Makes 4 servings

This dish is perfect for late winter, which in our neck of woods means the cod are running. Cod caught in icy waters and delivered straight to the market is hard to beat for taste and value. Rather than buy spring produce from faraway lands at this time of year, we prefer to capitalize on the last of the winter vegetables. Savoy cabbage, with its dark green wrinkled leaves and nutty flavor, is one that always grabs our attention. It's excellent with the fish.

Four 8-ounce skinless cod fillets, about 1 inch thick, or snapper

Peanut oil

Kosher salt

Freshly ground black pepper

½ pound new potatoes, scrubbed and sliced ½ inch thick

¼ pound slab bacon

1 small head Savoy cabbage, cored and cut into 1-inch dice (about 1½ pounds)

1 cup Chicken Broth, preferably homemade (page 53), or low-sodium canned broth

2 tablespoons unsalted butter

½ cup thinly sliced fresh chives or scallions

1. Heat the oven to 425°F.

2. Brush the fillets lightly with oil and sprinkle with salt and pepper. Arrange them on a foil-lined baking sheet and let stand at room temperature while preparing the vegetables.

3. Toss the potatoes with 2 tablespoons of oil and salt and pepper to taste in a large bowl until coated with the oil. Arrange the slices in a single layer on a separate baking sheet and bake until golden brown and tender, about 20 minutes.

4. Cut away the skin from the bacon, if necessary, and cut the bacon into ½-inch cubes. Place in a large heavy pan over medium-low heat and cook, stirring occasionally, until the bacon is well browned and has rendered most of its fat. Remove the bacon to paper towels to drain and pour off all but a thin layer of the fat from the pan.

5. Increase the heat to medium. Add a handful of cabbage and stir until the cabbage begins to wilt. Add more cabbage to the pan. Keep stirring and adding cabbage whenever there is room in the pan until all the cabbage has been added. Increase the heat slightly and cook until the cabbage is lightly browned and tender, about 5 minutes. Season to taste with salt and pepper and set aside. *The cod and vegetables may be prepared to this point up to 1 day in advance and refrigerated separately. Bring to room temperature 30 minutes before baking.*

6. Bake the cod until just cooked through but still moist at the thickest part, about 10 minutes. Add the bacon, potatoes, broth, butter, and chives to the cabbage in the pan. Bring to a boil over high heat and cook until the liquid is reduced enough to coat the cabbage. Season to taste with salt and pepper.

7. Divide the cabbage mixture among 4 serving plates and top each with a cod fillet. Serve hot.

Lone Star Shrimp

Makes 4 servings

Corn, peppers, and chili powder spell Texas to us. These foil packets make terrific surprise packages for a party. To serve them as a main course, have your guests slit open the foil and let the contents tumble out next to a mound of Tomato Rice (page 221). For starters, make them half size. We often transport a crate of pint-size packets to a barbecue, pop them into the oven upon arrival, and serve them, still in the wrapper, while we get the main act going on the grill.

2 cups fresh corn kernels (about 3 ears corn) or frozen kernels

½ cup roasted red pepper strips

1 large or 2 small jalapeño peppers, stemmed, seeded, and thinly sliced

1 pound large (21 to 25 per pound) shrimp, peeled and deveined (page 41)

1 tablespoon olive oil

2 teaspoons fresh lime juice

½ teaspoon chili powder or ground cumin

½ teaspoon kosher salt

1. Put the corn in a bowl, add the pepper strips and jalapeño, and toss. Put the shrimp in a separate bowl, add the olive oil, lime juice, chili powder, and a sprinkling of salt, and toss.

2. Tear off 4 pieces of aluminum foil, each 20 inches long. Fold each sheet in half lengthwise and turn it so the short side is parallel to the edge of the work surface. For each packet, place a mound of the corn mixture in the center of the lower half. Top the corn with a row of shrimp. Fold the far half of the foil toward you over the corn and shrimp. Double crease the 3 open sides tightly to seal in the filling. *The packets may be prepared to this point up to 6 hours in advance and refrigerated. Remove from the refrigerator 30 minutes before cooking.*

3. Place the oven rack in the lowest position and heat the oven to 400°F.

4. Place the packets in a single layer on a baking sheet and bake for 8 minutes. At this point the shrimp should be cooked through. To be sure, open one of the packets and test the shrimp by cutting into the thickest part before opening the remaining packets. Reseal the open package and cook for 1 to 2 minutes more if necessary. Serve immediately.

Saffron Seafood Stew

Makes 6 servings

Don't let the long list of ingredients intimidate you. This is a speedy dish and a perfect one for a crowd. All of the cooking —except for the fish—can be done up to two days ahead; then it takes less than ten minutes to finish the dish. Serve the stew with Red Onion Bread (page 24) and/or Walnut-Basil Bread (page 25) and a big tossed salad.

1½ cups chopped tomato, canned or fresh

1 pound small red potatoes, scrubbed and thinly sliced

1 large red onion, cut in half and thinly sliced

10 cloves garlic

2 cups water

1 cup dry white wine

1 teaspoon kosher salt

½ teaspoon (lightly packed) saffron threads (see Note)

¼ cup chopped fresh parsley

½ cup mayonnaise

¼ teaspoon crushed red pepper

1½ pounds firm fish fillets, such as swordfish, halibut, cod, snapper, or grouper, preferably two or more types (see Note)

18 large shrimp or mussels or small clams (see Note)

1. Combine the tomato, potatoes, onion, garlic, water, wine, salt, and saffron in a large nonreactive pot. Bring to a boil over high heat, reduce the heat, and simmer, covered, until the potatoes are tender but still firm, about 10 minutes. Stir in the parsley and remove from the heat.

2. Combine the mayonnaise and crushed red pepper in a blender jar. Add 3 tablespoons of the liquid and 4 of the garlic cloves from the stew base in Step 1. Blend until smooth. *The stew base and sauce can be prepared to this point up to 2 days in advance and refrigerated, covered, separately.*

3. Cut the fish fillets into cubes about 2 inches each. You may leave the skin on.

4. Reheat the stew base to a simmer over low heat. Add the fish and shellfish, cover the pot, and cook until the fish is cooked through and the shrimp has turned pink (or the shells of the clams or mussels have opened), about 5 minutes. Check the seasoning. Remove from the heat and stir a few spoons of the liquid into the mayonnaise sauce. Transfer the stew to a serving bowl and pour some of the sauce over the top. Serve immediately, passing the remaining sauce.

Notes: If saffron threads are not available, use ¼ teaspoon powdered saffron.

Substitute squid, cleaned and cut up, or scallops for some of the fish, if desired.

If you leave the shells on the shrimp, they will taste better and add to the appearance of the stew, but some people may find them difficult to handle. To peel and devein the shrimp, see page 41.

Scrub the clams and mussels thoroughly with a stiff brush under cold running water. Pull off the beards of the mussels just before cooking.

Vegetables, Beans, and Grains

Life was simpler in the old days when eateries bore names like Epicure Diner and plates were divided into sections for meat, mashed, and vege. Or two veges. We blinked, and the Blue Plate Special, the era of compartments, was gone. Now it's Blue Collar Food and endless choice.

Should the vegetables be roasted, pureed, or baked in a gratin today? The beans enlivened with greens or brightened with fresh peppers? Rice flavored with coconut or curry? How about tabbouleh or couscous instead?

In this chapter, we've collected recipes for some of our most popular vegetable, bean, and grain dishes, "sides" in restaurant parlance. But we don't like to call them that because we consider it a misnomer——many of these dishes can easily serve as a meal-in-one with a salad or as one dish in a meal of sides.

With some of the recipes, we've made suggestions for mixing and matching them with others in the book. But often we leave it to your personal inclination. Over time, we've developed some simple guidelines to help us create the kind of harmonious combination of flavors and textures that makes a satisfying meal. We always consider presentation as well—how the food looks, that is, colors, shapes, and arrangement on the plate. Here are a few of our rules of thumb:

- Be sure to serve something to soak up the sauce or gravy with juicy main dishes.
- Don't be afraid to pair dishes with full-blown flavor with plain main dishes.
- Be careful to pair dishes with delicate flavor with main dishes that don't overwhelm it.
- Keep close to the ethnic origins when matching dishes from around the world. You don't want World War III to break out on the plate.
- Avoid johnny-one-note meals—all green food, cilantro on everything, nothing you can sink your teeth into.
- Remember that if a combination seems odd, it probably is. Think twice.

Vegetables

Nobody ever had to bribe or threaten us to make us eat our vegetables. We love them, now more than ever since there are so many unusual ones on the market. It isn't so long ago, after all, that you had to chase down vegetables like fennel, broccoli rabe, and green cauliflower in ethnic neighborhoods or pricey specialty markets.

Besides the vegetable dishes in the pages that follow, you will find vegetables combined with pasta in Orzo Faux Risotto (page 118), with beans in White Beans and Kale (page 216), and in our salads and soups. We urge you to try them all.

Roasted Asparagus

Makes 4 servings

When we cater an outdoor party, we make an edible centerpiece of roasted vegetables, using whatever we find in the market that day. We're even willing to include less-than-perfect tomatoes, which benefit greatly from roasting (page 209). We always try to get some asparagus, partly because they look so nice, partly because people can eat them with their fingers. An assortment of roasted vegetables also makes a great open sandwich on French bread slathered with Grainy Mustard Mayonnaise (page 29). You can use this recipe as a guide for roasting other tender vegetables. The method remains the same, but the cooking time will vary.

1½ pounds medium asparagus (about 32 spears)

2 tablespoons olive oil, preferably extra virgin

1 teaspoon kosher salt

Pinch freshly ground black pepper

Lemon or orange wedges

1. Heat the oven to 425°F.

2. Bend each asparagus spear until it snaps. Discard the tougher bottom part and place the tops in a large mixing bowl. Pour the olive oil over the asparagus, sprinkle them with salt and pepper, and toss to coat. Spread the asparagus in a single layer on a heavy baking sheet.

3. Roast until the asparagus is browned and tender, about 15 minutes. Remove and cool to room temperature before serving. Pass wedges of lemon or orange separately.

Signor Mario's Baked Cauliflower

Makes 4 servings

We had the pleasure of spending some time in the kitchens of Regaleali, a wine and olive oil-producing estate in Sicily owned by the Tasca family. The Marchesa Anna Tasca Lanza runs a cooking school there, demonstrating traditional cooking of the region. In the main kitchen, the family's _monzù,_ Mario Lo Menzo, prepares the daily meals for her parents, the Count and Countess Lanza; he relies almost exclusively on food produced or raised on the estate. (_Monzù_ is a centuries-old title given to chefs who complete rigorous training in both classical French and traditional southern Italian cooking. Only one _monzù_ may confer the title of _monzù_ on another. Signor Mario is the last of a long line of _monzùs_ in Sicily.) This recipe is from the refined country cooking end of Signor Mario's repertoire rather than the baronial side and features one of his favorite tricks—adding a little water to sautéed onions. This "takes out some of the fire," as he says, and makes them a mellow addition to this and many other vegetable dishes.

1 medium head cauliflower, preferably green cauliflower

⅓ cup olive oil, preferably extra virgin

2 medium red onions, finely chopped

¼ cup water

¼ cup pitted oil-cured black olives, finely chopped (see Note)

Kosher salt

Freshly ground black pepper

¼ cup dry breadcrumbs

2 to 3 tablespoons grated pecorino or parmesan

1. Remove the outer leaves and cut away any blemishes from the cauliflower. Cut away the large part of the cauliflower stem, leaving enough intact to hold the head of cauliflower together. If you prefer, you may cut the head of cauliflower into quarters before cooking. Cook the cauliflower in a large pot of boiling salted water until the core is tender when tested with a knife, about 10 to 12 minutes. Remove from the hot water with 2 large spoons and let the cauliflower drain briefly over the pot. Transfer to a colander in the sink and rinse under cold water until cool.

2. Empty the pot and dry it. Return it to medium heat. Add the olive oil and stir in the onions. Cook until they begin to turn transparent, about 4 to 5 minutes. Add the water and continue cooking, stirring occasionally, until the onions begin to brown around the edges, about 12 minutes. Remove the pot from the heat.

3. Cut the cauliflower into quarters if you didn't do so before cooking. Slice the cauliflower pieces about 1 inch thick. Add the cauliflower pieces and the olives to the pot, stir to mix well and check the seasonings. Add salt and pepper if necessary. Transfer the mixture to a baking dish in which the cauliflower fits in a single layer. Sprinkle the top of the cauliflower with the breadcrumbs and pecorino. *The cauliflower may be prepared to this point up to 1 day in advance. Cover and refrigerate. Let the cauliflower come to room temperature for 30 minutes before baking.*

4. Heat the oven to 350°F.

5. Bake the cauliflower until heated through and golden brown on top, about 35 minutes.

Note: Oil-cured olives are sold in small jars in many supermarkets or loose in specialty shops and Mediterranean groceries. You will need 1 to 2 ounces or about ⅓ cup of olives before pitting.

Fennel and Leek Gratin

Makes 4 servings

Making a classic gratin can be time consuming what with layering vegetables in a baking dish and pouring a precooked sauce over them. A Blue Collar gratin, on the other hand, is swift— just toss the ingredients together in a bowl and dump them into a baking dish. Trust us—it works! Let this recipe serve as a model: Choose vegetables that look good in the produce display and that suit your menu, clean and cut them up as necessary, and prepare the gratin as described in Step 4. The combination of fennel and leeks goes well with roasted or grilled meat—or fish—and, surprisingly, with braised dishes like Veal and Artichoke Stew (page 176). Let the sauces from the two run together on the plate.

2 large bulbs fennel (about 2½ pounds)

3 medium leeks

½ cup heavy cream

½ cup plus 1 tablespoon grated parmesan

Pinch grated nutmeg

1 teaspoon kosher salt

Large pinch freshly ground black pepper

1 tablespoon dried breadcrumbs

1.   Heat the oven to 350°F.

2.   Trim the stalks and root end from the fennel bulbs. Cut the bulbs in half, then into quarters. Trim away most of the core, leaving enough intact to hold the slices together. Cut the fennel into ¼-inch strips. Set aside.

3. Cut the dark green parts and the roots from the leeks and cut the white part of each leek in half lengthwise. Cut crosswise into ½-inch lengths. Place the leeks in a large bowl of cool water and swish them around to separate and remove the fine dirt between the layers. Drain, shaking well to remove as much water as possible. If necessary, rinse and drain again.

4. Combine the fennel, leeks, cream, ½ cup parmesan, nutmeg, salt, and pepper in 9 × 9-inch baking dish and stir until well mixed. Mix together the remaining parmesan and the breadcrumbs and sprinkle over the top. Bake, uncovered, until the top is golden brown and the fennel is tender, about 45 minutes. Serve hot.

Note: Fresh fennel, sometimes called anise, is available through most of the cooler months. The root can be cooked or eaten raw as a crudité or thinly sliced in salads. The feathery fronds are very good snipped fine in soups, stews, and salads.

Vegetables, Beans, and Grains

195

Roasted Broccoli

Makes 4 servings

For broccoli lovers only! Roasting intensifies the flavor of all vegetables, broccoli in particular. Leftover roasted broccoli is delicious chopped and tossed into hot or cold pasta dishes.

1½ pounds broccoli

3 tablespoons extra virgin olive oil

Kosher salt

Freshly ground black pepper

2 tablespoons fresh lemon juice

1. Heat the oven to 350°F.

2. Cut off and discard 2 to 3 inches of the thick lower stems of the broccoli. Cut the tops lengthwise into spears of roughly the same size. Place the broccoli in a bowl and toss with the olive oil, salt, and pepper. Arrange the broccoli in a single layer in a 13 × 9-inch baking dish.

3. Bake until the stems are tender, 30 to 35 minutes. Sprinkle with lemon juice and serve.

Mushrooms have, er, mushroomed in the marketplace in the past few years. So many wild and unusual varieties have become available, sautéed mushrooms should no longer be relegated to the top of a steak. For a superb side dish, mix some of the so-called wild mushrooms —most are actually cultivated nowadays— with domestic button mushrooms. The firmer ones, like shiitakes (caps only) and cremini, should be sliced thinner than button mushrooms; softer ones, like oyster mushrooms, somewhat thicker. Sauté the mushrooms until they start to brown. Flip and toss them in the pan and listen to them squeak. They're telling you they're ready.

- 3 tablespoons unsalted butter
- 1 pound button mushrooms, wiped clean and cut into quarters, or assorted fresh mushrooms, wiped clean, trimmed, and cut into 2-inch pieces
- 2 tablespoons chopped fresh parsley
- 1 teaspoon finely chopped garlic
- 2 tablespoons lemon juice
- Kosher salt
- Freshly ground black pepper

Heat 2 tablespoons of the butter in a large skillet, preferably nonstick, over medium heat until it begins to bubble. Add the mushrooms and cook, stirring occasionally, until they begin to brown and all the liquid in the skillet is absorbed, 3 to 4 minutes. Stir the remaining butter, the parsley, garlic, and lemon juice together in a small bowl. Add to the mushrooms and cook for 1 minute, stirring well. Season to taste with salt and pepper and transfer the mushrooms to a serving dish. Serve hot.

Roasted New Potatoes with Garlic

Makes 4 servings

This is not a dainty dish. The cloves of garlic are little flavor packets to be squeezed onto the potatoes. Roasting garlic, remember, transforms it into a mellow condiment with only a faint memory of its raw wallop.

1¼ pounds white or red new potatoes, about 2 inches in diameter (8 to 10 potatoes)

2 tablespoons olive oil plus some for the baking dish

8 or more cloves garlic, unpeeled but extra "paper" removed

2 tablespoons fresh rosemary leaves (see Note)

1 teaspoon kosher salt

Freshly ground black pepper

1. Heat oven to 350°F. Lightly oil a baking dish, in which the potatoes will fit in a single layer, with some of the olive oil.

2. Scrub the potatoes well. Quarter them and place in a large bowl. Pour the olive oil over the potatoes and add the garlic, rosemary, salt, and pepper to taste. Toss until the potatoes and garlic are coated with oil and seasonings. Turn the potatoes into the baking dish.

3. Roast until the potatoes are browned and the garlic is very tender, about 45 minutes, stirring occasionally. Serve the potatoes hot, squeezing the pulp from the roasted garlic cloves onto the potatoes or bread.

Note: Four teaspoons dried rosemary can be substituted for the fresh. Put the rosemary in a small heatproof bowl and pour in some boiling water. Let stand for 5 minutes and drain before using.

We should all be grateful to the lazy fellow who first thought of not peeling the potatoes for mashing. This dish is the antithesis of silky mashed potatoes. For a carbo version of the ice-cream parlor fold-in, stir in some crumbled bacon, corn kernels, finely chopped sundried tomatoes, or leftover Blue Collar Black Bean Salad (page 218) — whatever catches your fancy.

12 medium red new potatoes (about 1½ pounds)

4 tablespoons (½ stick) unsalted butter

3 scallions, finely chopped

1 cup milk

1 tablespoon kosher salt

½ teaspoon freshly ground black pepper

1. Scrub the potatoes and cut into 1-inch cubes. Place in a large saucepan and pour in enough cold water to cover by 2 inches. Bring the water to a boil over high heat, reduce the heat, and simmer, uncovered, until the potatoes are tender, about 15 minutes.

2. While the potatoes are cooking, heat the butter in a small saucepan over low heat. When the butter is melted, add the scallions and cook until softened, about 2 minutes. Add the milk and cook just until heated through. Remove from the heat.

3. Drain the potatoes and transfer to a mixing bowl. Mash with a potato masher while gradually adding the milk mixture. Stop when the potatoes are the texture you like. Check the seasoning and add more salt, pepper, or butter if desired. Serve hot.

Blue Collar Mashed Potatoes

Makes 4 servings

For some people, a life without mashed potatoes is a life not worth living. We count many such among our clients, and so we've perfected this very smooth puree and even devised a way to make it ahead and reheat it without any loss of flavor (see Note). If you prefer your mashed potatoes with lumps, use a masher instead of the potato ricer or food mill.

2¼ pounds russet potatoes, peeled and sliced 1 inch thick (about 4 medium potatoes)

¾ cup milk, buttermilk, or skim milk

6 tablespoons (¾ stick) unsalted butter

Kosher salt

Freshly ground black pepper

1. Place the potatoes in a large saucepan with enough salted cold water to cover. Bring to a boil over high heat, reduce the heat, and simmer until the potatoes are tender, about 15 minutes. Drain and return the potatoes to the empty pot. Cover and let stand for 5 minutes.

2. Heat the milk and butter in a small pan over low heat until the butter is melted.

3. Pass the potatoes through a potato ricer or a food mill fitted with the fine blade into a bowl. Beat in the hot milk mixture and add salt and pepper to taste. Serve hot.

Note: Mashed potatoes can be made up to 45 minutes ahead and kept warm in a heatproof container in a warm (250°F.) oven or the potatoes can be mashed up to 4 hours in advance. Turn them into a baking dish, let cool to room temperature, and refrigerate, covered with aluminum foil. Reheat the potatoes, covered, in a 350°F. oven until very hot, about 35 minutes.

Mashed Potatoes with Chives: Add ½ cup thinly sliced fresh chives along with the milk and butter in Step 3.

Mashed Potatoes with Roasted Garlic and Olive Oil: Substitute 4 tablespoons olive oil for the butter and add 3 tablespoons roasted garlic puree (page 202) to the potatoes after passing them through the ricer or food mill.

To Roast Garlic

Heat the oven to 375° F. Choose a small, deep baking dish. Cut off the pointed tip of the garlic head with a serrated knife. Rub off all the papery outer layers, leaving the cloves attached. Place the garlic cut side up in the baking dish. Spoon enough olive oil over the garlic to coat it lightly. Pour in enough chicken broth (homemade or canned) or water to fill the dish to ½ inch. Cover the dish tightly with aluminum foil.

Bake until tender, about 45 minutes. Check the baking dish; the liquid level should remain the same—add liquid as necessary. Remove the aluminum foil and continue baking until the cloves are lightly browned, about 10 minutes.

Serve the garlic warm as a side dish—pull off individual garlic cloves and squeeze out the soft pulp with your fingers.

To store for use in other dishes, squeeze all the pulp from the garlic, pack it (without air spaces) into a small glass or ceramic jar and cover the top with a thin layer of olive oil. Store it in the refrigerator for up to two weeks.

Why not? Mashed sweets don't take to gravies like regular mashed potatoes — they have too much personality for that — but they are quite wonderful with unsauced meats like Grilled Chicken Breasts (page 134) and Grilled Pork Chops Teriyaki (page 135).

2 pounds sweet potatoes (about 4 medium)

1 cup milk

4 tablespoons (½ stick) unsalted butter

Large pinch nutmeg, preferably freshly grated

1 teaspoon kosher salt

¼ teaspoon freshly ground black pepper

Peel the sweet potatoes and slice them about 1 inch thick. Boil in plenty of salted water until very tender, about 25 minutes. Heat the milk, butter, nutmeg, salt, and pepper to simmering over low heat and remove from the heat. Drain the sweet potatoes well and pass them through a potato ricer or mash them with a potato masher. Beat in the hot milk mixture, check the seasoning, and serve hot.

Vegetables, Beans, and Grains

Butternut Squash Puree

Makes 4 servings

Hard squash is one of the consolations of a northern winter. Sweet and rich in taste, butternut (or acorn or Hubbard) squash makes the kind of stick-to-the-ribs side dish you crave when the days grow short and the weather dismal.

1 butternut squash (about 2½ pounds)
Vegetable oil
2 tablespoons unsalted butter
1¼ teaspoons kosher salt
¼ teaspoon freshly ground black pepper
Large pinch grated nutmeg

1.   Heat the oven to 375°F. Lightly oil a heavy baking sheet.

2.   Cut the squash in half lengthwise with a serrated knife and scoop out the seeds. Brush lightly with vegetable oil. Place the halves, cut side down, on the baking sheet. Bake until the underside is well browned and the squash is very tender at the thickest point when poked with a knife, about 1 hour. Remove and let the squash stand until cool enough to handle.

3.   Peel the skin away (it should come off easily) and transfer the squash to a heavy saucepan. Cook, mashing with a potato masher or wire whisk, until most of the liquid, if any, is evaporated and the squash is a coarse puree. Remove the pan from the heat and whisk in the butter, salt, pepper, and nutmeg. Serve hot. *The squash can be prepared completely in advance and refrigerated. Reheat in a heavy saucepan over very low heat or in a baking dish in a 250°F. oven.*

Note: Toast the squash seeds for a special treat. Rinse them well, picking off the fibers, and drain on paper towels. When they are completely dry, toss with a little oil, salt, and pepper—plus chili powder or curry powder if you like—and toast in a 350°F. oven until crisp, about 6 to 7 minutes.

Creamed Spinach

Makes 4 servings

Spinach, fortunately, is one of the few vegetables that can withstand the rigors of deep freezing. We take advantage of the convenience of the frozen stuff in this dish, which can be made in no time. Keep in mind, though, that the spinach soaks up an amazing amount of cream. This is an all-or-nothing proposition. If you're counting calories and cholesterol, you'd better stick to steamed fresh spinach with a chaste squeeze of lemon.

Two 10-ounce packages frozen chopped spinach, thawed

1 cup heavy cream

1 tablespoon unsalted butter

2 teaspoons kosher salt

½ teaspoon freshly ground black pepper

Pinch grated nutmeg

2 tablespoons grated parmesan (optional)

Squeeze out the spinach with your hands to remove as much water as possible. Bring the cream, butter, salt, pepper, and nutmeg to a boil in a small saucepan over medium heat. Add the spinach and stir until coated and heated through. Stir in the parmesan, if using, taste, and adjust the seasonings if necessary. Serve hot.

Note: For a creamier consistency, transfer about a third of the creamed spinach to a blender and pulse until almost smooth. Stir this mixture back into the rest.

Baked Creamed String Beans

Makes 4 servings

We were trying to decide whether to add string beans or creamed onions to our menu for Thanksgiving one season when Bill hit on this idea. The dish has a wonderful homey quality and can be assembled completely in advance, always a boon for Thanksgiving or any other time you're feeding a crowd.

¾ pound string beans

1½ tablespoons unsalted butter

1 small onion, thinly sliced

1½ tablespoons all-purpose flour

1 cup hot milk

Large pinch grated nutmeg

Kosher salt

Freshly ground black pepper

2 tablespoons dry breadcrumbs

2 tablespoons grated parmesan

1. Cut both ends from the beans. Cook them in a large pot of boiling salted water until tender and bright green, about 6 minutes. Drain in a colander and rinse under cold water until completely cooled. Drain well.

2. Heat the butter in a small saucepan over medium heat until bubbling. Stir in the onion and cook, stirring occasionally, until light golden, about 5 minutes. Stir in the flour and continue cooking, stirring constantly, for 2 minutes. Pour the milk in slowly while stirring constantly. Add the nutmeg and salt and pepper to taste. Reduce the heat and simmer for 2 minutes. Arrange the beans in an even layer in a 9 × 9-inch baking dish and pour the sauce over them. Stir the breadcrumbs and cheese together in a small bowl. Sprinkle this mixture over the beans. *The beans may be prepared to this point 1 day in advance. Bring the dish to room temperature for 30 minutes before baking.*

3. Heat the oven to 375°F.

4. Bake the beans until they are heated through, the sauce is bubbling, and the topping is golden brown, about 20 minutes. Serve hot.

Succotash

Makes 4 servings

Succotash is one of those dishes you just don't understand when you're a kid. But with age comes wisdom. (Well, sometimes.) If it's been a while since you gave succotash a try, follow this easy recipe, developed with the best and freshest corn of the season in mind. Be open-minded.

2 tablespoons unsalted butter

3 scallions thinly sliced, green and white parts separated

One 10-ounce package frozen lima beans, defrosted and drained (about 2 cups)

2 cups corn kernels (about 3 ears fresh corn)

¾ cup water, or as needed

1 teaspoon kosher salt

Freshly ground black pepper

Melt the butter in a heavy large skillet over medium heat. Add the white part of the scallions and cook until wilted, about 2 minutes. Add the lima beans, corn, ¾ cup water, salt, and pepper to taste. Cover the skillet and cook until the vegetables are tender, about 15 minutes. Stir occasionally and check the liquid in the skillet. If necessary, add 1 or 2 tablespoons water. Stir in the scallion greens, check for seasoning, and serve hot. *The succotash can be prepared entirely up to 1 day in advance and refrigerated. Reheat over low heat.*

Tomatoes Provençal

Makes 4 Servings

When your tomatoes have not baked long enough on the vine under the sun, stick them in the oven and let them bake there. They'll acquire an intense, smoky flavor that is good with roasted or grilled meat or fish or other roasted vegetables. And they are decorative. Which is not to say you shouldn't prepare this dish with dead-of-August vine-ripened tomatoes— they'll be even better.

2 ripe but firm tomatoes (about 1 pound)

Kosher salt

¼ cup dried breadcrumbs

2 tablespoons chopped fresh basil

2 tablespoons olive oil, preferably extra virgin

1 teaspoon finely chopped garlic

Freshly ground black pepper

1. Heat the oven to 350°F. Core the tomatoes and cut them in half crosswise. Gently squeeze out the seeds. Sprinkle the cut sides of the tomato with salt and set them, cut side down, in a colander to drain for 5 to 10 minutes.

2. Combine the breadcrumbs, basil, olive oil, and garlic in a small bowl. Mix with a fork until well blended. Season to taste with pepper.

3. Place the tomatoes, cut side up, in a baking dish in which they fit comfortably. Divide the topping evenly among the tomatoes. *The tomatoes may be prepared to this point up to 1 day in advance.*

4. Bake until the tomatoes are soft and the topping is golden brown, about 25 minutes. Transfer carefully to serving plates. Serve hot or at room temperature.

Life without beans would be very dull indeed. There is a staggering variety of dried beans on the market, with new ones making an appearance every day, or so it seems. Recipes come to us from all over the world. If we tried them all, we'd be eating beans every day of the year, without ever repeating a dish.

In addition, beans are cheap, nutritious, convenient, and easy to cook. Why then are they perceived as troublesome? The need to soak beans is a deterrent for some; for those we propose our "power soak" (page 212). The flatus factor inhibits others; for those we propose an ancient remedy—adding lemon juice or vinegar toward the end of the cooking time. The notion that beans are poor man's food discourages still others; for this last group, we offer a selection of stylish bean dishes that can be served without shame or apology on almost any occasion.

Lentils,
Hot or Cold

Makes 4 servings

Lentils come in many sizes and colors, from pink to almost black. Tuck a couple of bags of them in the cupboard for an amazing quick fix. Unlike true beans, lentils do not need to be soaked, and they are done in about half an hour, even less for pink and "split" lentils. You can use this recipe with any kind of lentils to prepare a hearty side dish for roasts or a room-temperature salad.

1½ cups lentils (about two thirds of a 1-pound bag)

3 tablespoons olive oil or vegetable oil

2 small ribs celery, finely diced

1 small onion, finely diced

1 carrot, peeled and finely diced

3 cups water

1 teaspoon kosher salt

¼ teaspoon freshly ground black pepper

3 scallions, trimmed and thinly sliced

2 tablespoons fresh lemon juice

1. Rinse the lentils in a colander under cold running water. Heat 1 tablespoon of the oil in a medium heavy saucepan over medium heat. Add the celery, onion, and carrot and stir until the vegetables are softened and lightly browned, about 5 minutes. Add the lentils, water, salt, and pepper. Increase the heat to high and bring to a boil. Reduce the heat and simmer the lentils, uncovered, until tender and just about all of the liquid is absorbed, about 30 minutes. Stir occasionally to prevent the lentils from sticking. If necessary, add small amounts of water to the pan to keep the lentils moist.

2. Remove the pan from the heat and beat in the remaining 2 tablespoons of olive oil, the scallions, and lemon juice with a wire whisk or wooden spoon, creating a very coarse puree. Check the lentils for seasoning. Serve hot.

Variation

To serve as a salad, let the lentils cool to room temperature and season to taste with olive oil and lemon juice. The lentils may need additional salt as well.

How to Cook Beans

Once dried, true beans (navy beans, kidney beans, pintos, black or turtle beans, chick peas or garbanzos, etc.) need to be soaked. Lentils are not true beans, although we've include them in this chapter, and do not need to be soaked. Though very tempting to skip, this step is essential. Without it, you risk unevenly cooked, mealy beans or beans that never get tender.

Overnight soak. This is the easiest way to soak beans—if only you remember. Wash and pick over the beans, put them in a deep container, and add cold water to cover the beans by about 2 inches. Leave the beans to soak in a cool place for at least 12 hours, preferably 24 hours. If your kitchen is very warm, and you want to soak the beans for a full 24 hours, refrigerate the beans while soaking. Drain and rinse the beans before continuing with the recipe.

Power soak. Nobody's perfect—even old pros like us sometimes forget—so we sometimes give the beans a power soak, a term we coined for quick soaking. To do this, wash and pick over the beans and put them in a large pot. Add 3 times their volume of cold water, bring to a boil, and boil for 1 minute. Remove from the heat and let stand for 1 hour. Drain and rinse the beans before continuing with the recipe.

Cooking the beans is almost as simple as soaking them. Here are a few pointers:

- Cover the beans with cold unsalted water and slowly bring to a simmer. Skim off any foam that rises to the surface.
- Add chopped aromatic vegetables (onion, carrot, and celery) to the beans once the foaming has stopped. Or, for even more flavor, sauté the vegetables in olive oil or butter first, then add the beans and water.
- Gently simmer the beans until tender.
- Add herbs and spices—parsley, fresh or dried sage or thyme, bay leaf, ground cumin or coriander, etc.— while the beans are simmering.
- Add salt about two thirds of the way through the cooking.
- Add lemon juice or vinegar at the end. Taste and adjust the seasoning to balance the lemon juice or vinegar and salt flavors.

Canned beans. These are fine for many dishes, especially those where the texture and appearance of whole beans are not important, but they are not an across-the-board substitute for dried beans. We often use canned beans— for a crostini topping (page 33), for Hummus (page 36), in Black Bean Burritos (page 26), and in Fusilli and White Bean Casserole (page 112), as well as the Baked Chick Pea Casserole and Refried Beans, Italian Style in this chapter. We recommend you keep an assortment of canned beans on hand for emergencies. Cannellini, chick peas, and white beans are particularly versatile.

Baked Chick Pea Casserole

Makes 6 servings

Suddenly chick peas became chic. We didn't mind—we'd been eating them all along, sometimes for days at a time. This casserole, a longtime favorite, is good as a side dish with chicken or pork. Leftovers, if any, can be reheated and spooned over Brown Rice Pilaf (page 224) or mashed with some tomato sauce or chicken broth to make a pasta sauce.

Canned chick peas are fine for this dish; they can be quickly tossed together with other pantry staples, baked, and on the table in just about half an hour.

Two 15-ounce cans chick peas (garbanzo beans), drained and rinsed
One 14½-ounce can whole tomatoes, coarsely chopped, with their
    liquid
1 small red onion, thinly sliced
2 tablespoons olive oil
2 cloves garlic, minced
½ teaspoon ground cumin
Kosher salt
Freshly ground black pepper
3 tablespoons dried breadcrumbs

1. Heat the oven to 375°F.

2. Combine the chick peas, tomatoes, onion, olive oil, garlic, cumin, and salt and pepper to taste. Stir until the onion slices are broken up and the ingredients are evenly mixed. Pour the mixture into an 11-inch oval or 8-inch square baking dish. The chick peas should be at least 1 inch deep and come to within 1 inch of the top of the dish. Sprinkle the breadcrumbs over the top.

3. Bake until the casserole is bubbling and the breadcrumbs are golden brown, about 25 minutes. If the crumbs are not browning, pass the dish under the broiler. Let the casserole stand for 5 minutes before serving.

A lighter version of the Mexican classic, these beans are great with Rosemary-Lemon Roasted Chicken (156) and Grilled Butterflied Leg of Lamb (140). Use them any time when you would otherwise serve mashed potatoes. It's also a perfect emergency side dish as all the ingredients can be kept on hand.

Two 19-ounce cans cannellini beans

2 tablespoons olive oil, preferably extra virgin

2 cloves garlic, very thinly sliced

1 teaspoon dried sage

½ cup water

2 teaspoons kosher salt

½ cup grated parmesan (optional)

Rinse the beans and drain thoroughly. Combine the oil, garlic, and sage in a small saucepan and heat over medium-low heat just until the garlic begins to brown. Quickly stir in the beans, water, and salt. Cook, stirring the beans and mashing them with a fork, until the beans have absorbed the water and are heated through. Stir in the parmesan, if desired. Serve hot.

Note: The beans may seem too thin at first, but they absorb the water fast.

White Beans and Kale

Makes 6 servings

Greens of every description have flooded the produce markets in recent years. Their distinctive, somewhat bitter flavor has wide appeal. We particularly like kale in this dish, but if it doesn't look sprightly, use escarole or chard. Serve this as a side dish with grilled or broiled meat — it's very nice with Grilled Chicken Breasts (page 134) — or as a meal-in-one.

¾ pound navy beans or baby lima beans (1½ cups)

2 inner ribs celery, with leaves, chopped

1 medium carrot, peeled and chopped

1 medium onion, chopped

1 bay leaf

2 cups water, or as needed

2 teaspoons kosher salt

2 tablespoons olive oil

2 pounds kale or escarole or Swiss chard

2 tablespoons fresh lemon juice

Freshly ground black pepper

1.   Soak the beans as described on page 212.

Drain and rinse the beans. Put them in a large pot and add the celery, carrot, onion, bay leaf, and water. Heat to a boil, reduce the heat, cover, and simmer, stirring occasionally, for 45 minutes.

Add the salt and olive oil. Check the liquid—there should be enough to barely cover the beans. If not, add water as necessary. Continue simmering, uncovered, until the beans are tender, about 15 minutes. Stir occasionally. *The beans may be prepared to this point up to 1 day in advance. Cool to room temperature and refrigerate. Heat the beans to a simmer before continuing with the recipe, adding water if necessary to return the beans to their original consistency.*

2. Cut the thick stems and any wilted or yellowed leaves from the kale and cut the leaves into pieces roughly 2 inches square. Wash the kale in 2 changes of cool water and drain thoroughly. Shake out as much water as possible from the leaves and dry well, preferably in a salad spinner.

3. Stir the lemon juice into the beans. Add the kale a handful at a time, stirring each until wilted before adding another. When all the kale has been added, simmer for 5 minutes. Check the seasoning, adding salt and pepper as necessary. Serve hot.

Blue Collar Black Bean Salad

Makes 4 servings

Perfect for barbecues, especially as a sidekick for Grilled Chili-rubbed Flank Steak (page 136). If you have any leftovers, use them to fill omelets or fold them into Mashed Red Potatoes (page 199).

6 ounces black or turtle beans (1 cup)

Kosher salt

3 tablespoons peanut or vegetable oil

1½ tablespoons fresh lemon juice

⅓ cup finely diced roasted red and/or yellow peppers (page 219) or
    bottled roasted red peppers (see Note)

3 scallions, very thinly sliced

Freshly ground black pepper

1. Soak the beans as described on page 212. Drain and rinse the beans. Transfer them to a small heavy saucepan. Pour in cold water to cover by 4 inches. Heat to a boil, reduce the heat, and simmer for 30 minutes. Add 1 tablespoon salt and continue to simmer until the beans are tender but still firm, about 15 minutes. Drain, rinse briefly under cold running water, and drain thoroughly.

2. Beat the oil and lemon juice in a large bowl until blended. Add the beans, peppers, and scallions. Season to taste with pepper. Toss to coat with dressing. Let stand for 30 minutes to 1 hour, tossing occasionally. Check the seasoning before serving. *The salad can be prepared entirely up to 1 day in advance and refrigerated. Bring the salad to room temperature and check the seasonings before serving.*

Note: Look for fire-roasted peppers rather than simple peeled red peppers or pimientos.

To Roast Peppers

Choose thick-fleshed, straight-sided yellow, red, or green bell peppers. Light a burner of your gas stove. (Use more burners for roasting more peppers.) Place the peppers directly over the flame and roast them until the skin is evenly blackened on all sides. Turn the peppers with a pair of long-handled tongs just as each side turns black, to prevent the peppers from overcooking. (Roasting the peppers can be done over hot coals, too.)

Place the blackened peppers in a heavy brown paper bag and close the bag. Or place the peppers in a bowl large enough to hold them comfortably and cover the bowl tightly with plastic wrap. Let the peppers stand until cool. The steam formed by covering the hot peppers will loosen the skins and make them easier to remove.

Cut the peppers in half and scrape out the seeds and liquid. Turn the peppers over and scrape off the blackened skins. At this point the peppers can be cut for use in recipes or stored in the refrigerator for up to 4 days, covered with a thin layer of olive oil.

Rice and Other Grains

Maybe it's because of all the plain white rice we ate as kids, but both of us prefer flavored rice. (Sorry, Mom!) We find our customers do too. White and brown rice pilafs—as well as tabbouleh and couscous—dress up the buffet table and add another dimension to the saucy stews we favor in winter and the straightforward grilled meats around which we plan barbecues in summer.

These dishes are all quick to fix, with a minimum of fuss. They are just as suited to one or two people as to a crowd. Leftovers will not suffer if reheated in the microwave, or they can be easily transformed into a main-dish salad by the addition of a little meat or chicken, also left over.

We're also partial to polenta. Contrary to most expert opinion, we've found it does not need lengthy preparation; that's a myth. Freshly made, with or without flavorings, polenta can function as a stand-in for mashed potatoes; it's great for sopping up a sauce. Any leftovers can be smoothed into a pan, refrigerated, and grilled the next day, as described on page 228. Polenta is also wonderful as a sort of supper porridge with a strong cheese, like one of the blues or feta, folded in.

So when you're shopping for the pantry, or for a siege, be sure to stock a supply of each of these: white and brown rice, preferably converted (not instant); bulgur; instant couscous; and coarse yellow cornmeal. You'll never be without a filling, wholesome grain dish for yourself and/or your friends again. Save wild rice, the very best you can afford, for special occasions.

At Blue Collar Foods, we like to add a little crunch and color to rice, so we use converted rice, which responds well to the pilaf treatment. Over the years, we have found it to be a no-fail proposition. If you prefer regular long-grain rice, by all means use that. It may need to be cooked a few minutes longer.

1 tablespoon vegetable oil or butter

2 ribs celery, finely diced

1 cup converted rice

1 cup Tomato Sauce, either homemade (page 95), or store-bought

1 cup water

½ teaspoon kosher salt

¼ teaspoon freshly ground black pepper

Heat the oil in a medium heavy saucepan over medium heat. Add the celery and cook, stirring, until lightly browned, about 4 minutes. Add the rice and stir to coat. Add the tomato sauce, water, salt, and pepper. Heat to a boil, reduce the heat to a bare simmer, and cover the pan. Cook until the rice is tender and the liquid absorbed, about 15 minutes. Check the seasoning and adjust if necessary. Serve hot.

Coconut Rice

Makes 6 servings

This dish erupted onto the Manhattan restaurant scene a couple of years back. Every fashionable chophouse in town seemed to have its version, which we usually found cloyingly sweet. So we set out to make our own. We think it's a winner.

1 tablespoon unsalted butter

½ cup sweetened shredded coconut

6 scallions, chopped

2½ cups water

½ cup half-and-half or light cream

1 tablespoon kosher salt

Large pinch freshly ground black pepper

1½ cups converted rice

Melt the butter in a large heavy saucepan over medium heat. Stir in the coconut and scallions and cook, stirring occasionally, until the coconut is lightly browned and the scallions are wilted, about 3 minutes. Add the water, half-and-half, salt, and pepper, increase the heat to high, and bring to a boil. Stir in the rice. Reduce the heat to a bare simmer, cover the pan, and cook, without stirring, until the rice is tender but still firm and the water is absorbed, about 15 minutes. Serve hot.

Note: If you use the sweetened coconut you find in the supermarket, the dish will be pleasantly sweet; if you use unsweetened coconut (available at health-food stores and specialty shops), it will be less sweet but seem more unctuous.

Curried Rice

Makes 6 servings

With just a fraction more effort than goes into cooking plain white rice, you can have a flavored rice that adds exponentially to the meal. Sometimes it can even be the meal, as in this case. Garnish the rice with any of the traditional curry condiments—raisins, chopped cucumber, chutney, and so on.

2 tablespoons vegetable oil

1 small white onion, finely diced

2 teaspoons curry powder, preferably Madras

1½ cups converted rice

3 cups water

2 teaspoons kosher salt

¼ cup plain yogurt

¼ cup finely chopped almonds, lightly toasted (see Note)

3 scallions, thinly sliced

1. Heat the oil in a medium heavy saucepan over medium heat. Add the onion and stir until wilted, about 4 minutes. Add the curry powder and cook for 1 minute. Add the rice and stir until coated. Pour in the water, increase the heat to high, and bring to a boil. Add the salt, give the rice a good stir, and adjust the heat so the liquid is at a bare simmer. Cover the pan and cook, without stirring, until the rice is tender but still firm and the liquid is absorbed, about 15 minutes.

2. Stir the yogurt, almonds, and scallions together in a small bowl. When the rice is cooked, remove the lid and stir in the yogurt mixture. Check for seasonings and serve hot.

Note: Toast the almonds in a small skillet over medium-low heat, stirring frequently, until golden brown, about 3 minutes. Remove immediately and let cool.

Brown Rice Pilaf

Makes 4 servings

Since brown rice takes longer to cook than white rice, it absorbs more of the other flavors in the pot. We use Uncle Ben's brown rice for our pilafs; it seems to hold up better than the plain. This is a good dish to serve with grilled and roasted meats.

1 tablespoon unsalted butter
1 tablespoon vegetable oil
1 medium carrot, peeled and finely diced
1 small onion, finely diced
1 medium rib celery, finely diced
1 cup Uncle Ben's brown rice
2 cups hot Chicken Broth, preferably homemade (page 53), or hot
    water
1½ teaspoons kosher salt (see Note)

Heat the butter and oil in a medium heavy saucepan over medium heat until the butter is bubbling. Stir in the carrot, onion, and celery and cook, stirring occasionally, until the vegetables begin to soften, about 5 minutes. Stir in the rice and stir until thoroughly mixed with the vegetables. Stir in the broth and salt. Increase the heat to high and bring to a boil. Immediately reduce the heat to a bare simmer. Give the rice a good stir, cover the pan, and simmer until the rice is tender and all the liquid is absorbed, about 45 minutes. Remove from the heat, and let stand, uncovered, for a few minutes before serving.

Note: Use less salt if using canned broth.

A festive dish to keep in mind for the holidays, whether for a buffet with baked ham or turkey or as a dressed-up partner for leftovers next day. The salad also makes an unusual stuffing for ripe tomatoes. Depending on how and where the wild rice was grown and harvested, it varies widely in price. For this dish, the more expensive kind is a must.

½ cup wild rice

1 cup broccoli florets

2 tablespoons fresh lemon juice

Kosher salt

Freshly ground black pepper

⅓ cup olive oil

1 large carrot, peeled and grated

⅓ cup finely chopped celery hearts, with leaves

1. Cook the wild rice in a medium heavy saucepan of gently boiling salted water until the rice is tender but still firm, about 25 to 30 minutes. Drain the rice and let it cool. Meanwhile cook the broccoli in a second pot of boiling salted water until tender but still firm, about 4 minutes. Drain the broccoli in a colander and rinse under cold running water to stop the cooking. Drain the broccoli very well.

2. Combine the lemon juice and salt and pepper to taste in a large bowl. Whisk while adding the oil in a thin stream. Continue whisking until all the oil is incorporated. Add the rice, broccoli, carrots, and celery and toss to coat with dressing. Check the seasoning and add salt and pepper to taste. Let the salad stand at room temperature for up to 1 hour or refrigerate for up to 6 hours before serving. Toss the salad and check the seasoning again before serving. *The salad can be prepared up to 1 day in advance and refrigerated, without adding the broccoli. Remove the salad about 30 minutes before serving, stir in the broccoli, and check the seasoning.*

Vegetables, Beans, and Grains

BCF Tabbouleh

Makes 8 servings

Tabbouleh, a Middle Eastern salad made with cracked wheat, is ideal picnic and barbecue food. It's light and refreshing, and it doesn't wilt in the heat. The Blue Collar version tones down the parsley and mint, which can drown out the nutty flavor of the wheat, and plays up the other traditional ingredients.

1 cup fine bulgur (cracked wheat)

2 cups boiling water

1 teaspoon kosher salt

1 small cucumber

2 plum tomatoes or 1 small tomato

3 tablespoons olive oil

2 tablespoons fresh lemon juice

2 small scallions, thinly sliced

1 tablespoon finely chopped fresh mint

¼ cup finely chopped parsley

1. Place the bulgur in a large heatproof bowl. Pour the boiling water over the bulgur, stir in the salt, and let it stand until softened but still firm, about 10 minutes. Drain, if necessary.

2. Peel the cucumber and cut it in half lengthwise. Scoop out and discard the seeds and finely dice the flesh. Core the tomatoes and cut them in half. Flick out most of the seeds and finely dice the tomato.

3. Combine the oil and lemon juice in a small bowl and beat until blended. Pour this over the bulgur and add the cucumber, tomato, scallions, mint, and parsley. Toss to combine. Check the seasoning and adjust if necessary. Let stand at least 30 minutes and check the seasoning again before serving. *The tabbouleh may be prepared up to 1 day in advance and refrigerated. Bring to room temperature and check the seasoning before serving.*

Parmesan Polenta

Makes 8 servings

Polenta is Italian for cornmeal mush. It is often served freshly cooked—it's a great companion for richly sauced dishes—but we prefer to make it ahead and let it cool until solid. Then we can slice it and grill or panfry it later. For parties, we flavor the polenta simply with parsley and parmesan; left to our own devices, we stir in some gorgonzola. These wedges go with virtually any roasted or grilled dish. They turn Sautéed Fresh Mushrooms (page 197) into a very special first course.

3 cups water

2 tablespoons unsalted butter

1½ tablespoons kosher salt

¼ teaspoon freshly ground black pepper

¾ cup yellow cornmeal, preferably coarse

2 tablespoons finely chopped parsley

¼ cup plus 3 tablespoons grated parmesan

Olive oil

1. Combine the water, butter, salt, and pepper in a medium heavy saucepan and bring to a boil over high heat. Add the cornmeal very gradually, stirring with a wire whisk. This should take about 2 minutes if you're doing it slowly enough. Cook, stirring constantly, until the cornmeal is tender and the consistency of oatmeal, about 3 minutes. Remove from the heat and stir in the parsley and parmesan. Immediately pour the polenta into an 8-inch metal pie pan, or another flameproof container of the same size. Let the polenta cool to warm. Cover the polenta with plastic wrap applied directly to the surface and refrigerate. *The polenta may be made to this point up to 2 days in advance.*

2.   Shortly before serving, remove the polenta from the refrigerator to room temperature for 30 minutes if necessary. Heat the broiler and place the broiler pan about 6 inches from the heat. Cut the polenta into 8 wedges. Brush the top of the polenta lightly with olive oil and sprinkle evenly with the remaining 3 tablespoons of parmesan. Broil until the top is golden brown, about 2 minutes. Serve hot.

Though strictly speaking a pasta, couscous cooks, looks, and tastes like a grain, very similar, in fact, to bulgur. It made the leap from Morocco, where it is prepared in a complicated, labor-intensive way, to the United States thanks to the development of instant couscous. The instant is idiot proof and ready in a flash. It's what you'll find on supermarket shelves. This dish goes particularly well with our Mediterranean Crossroads Lamb Shanks (page 178) and Veal and Artichoke Stew (page 176). If you have any couscous left over, toss it with olive oil and vinegar or lemon juice and serve it as a salad.

1 cup water

1 teaspoon kosher salt

Pinch freshly ground black pepper

⅛ teaspoon saffron threads (see Note)

½ cup frozen or shelled fresh peas

1 cup instant couscous

Heat the water, salt, pepper, and saffron to a simmer in a small saucepan over medium heat. Remove from the heat, cover the pan, and let stand for 10 minutes. Stir in the peas and reheat to a boil. Reduce the heat to a bare simmer and cook for 2 minutes, or until the peas are tender. Pour the couscous into a medium heatproof bowl and pour the hot saffron mixture over it. Cover with a plate or pot lid and let stand until the water is absorbed and the couscous is tender, about 5 minutes. Fluff the couscous with a fork and check the seasoning before serving.

Note: You may substitute powdered saffron for whole saffron threads; it is much less expensive. A large pinch should be enough to turn the water a deep shade of gold. If not, add a little more.

Desserts

For pastry chefs, one of the good things to emerge from the culinary turmoil of the past decade is a renewed appreciation of go-for-broke desserts. Paradoxically, at Blue Collar Food the demand is for the other kind, the old-fashioned type of dessert that Ma, or maybe Grandma, used to make. Perhaps people are tired of those architectural constructions that make you feel you need a degree in engineering to tackle.

We're asked for dessert platters that feature desserts that people can get their hands on, like slices of loaf cake, brownies, or unfrosted chocolate cake. For breakfast, whether it's served on china in the conference room of a Wall Street law firm or grabbed on the run at one of the coffee shops or espresso bars we supply, our clients want a piece of coffee cake or quick bread, and muffins, muffins, muffins. For parties, we're ready with what the Italians call spoon desserts—fresh or poached fruit, chocolate pudding and plate-and-fork cheesecakes, shortcakes, and pies. Never anything pretentious. Just Blue Collar Food.

Bill's wife's Aunt Elsie learned to bake as a little girl, and all her life it gave her pleasure to cook for other people. Her German mother handed down her mother's recipes for this rustic plum cake and Raisin-Walnut Coffee Cake, and we are handing them down to you.

Rich Pastry Dough (recipe follows)

6 large plums, such as friar, cut in half, or 12 Italian prune plums, pits
    removed

½ cup sugar

4 tablespoons (½ stick) unsalted butter, cut into small pieces

1.   Make the dough and line the baking pan with it or remove the pan from the refrigerator and let stand at room temperature for 30 minutes.

2.   Heat the oven to 350°F.

3.   Arrange the plums, cut side up, over the dough, pressing them gently into the dough. Sprinkle them evenly with sugar. Dot the top of the cake with butter.

4.   Bake until the crust is lightly browned, the plums are tender, and the juices are bubbling, about 45 minutes. Let the cake cool to warm or room temperature before cutting.

Rich Pastry Dough

One 11 × 7-inch crust

8 tablespoons (1 stick) unsalted butter, at room temperature

7 tablespoons sugar

2 large eggs

1 teaspoon vanilla extract

2 cups all-purpose flour

1 teaspoon baking powder

½ teaspoon kosher salt

Cream the butter and sugar in a small bowl with an electric mixer until light and fluffy. Continue beating while adding the eggs, one at a time. Beat well after each. Beat in the vanilla. Sift the flour, baking powder, and salt over the batter and fold them in to form a stiff batter. Lightly spray an 11 × 7-inch baking pan with vegetable spray. Press the dough into the pan to form an even layer in the bottom and about ½ inch up the sides. *The dough can be prepared to this point up to 1 day in advance, wrapped, and refrigerated. Remove from the refrigerator and let stand at room temperature for 30 minutes before adding the plums and baking.*

Fresh Fruit Cobbler

Makes 8 servings

In this old-fashioned cake, a lightly spiced batter rises up to envelop fresh fruit. Use whatever's in season——berries, pitted cherries, peaches, nectarines, apricots, apples, or pears, or a harmonious mix. Only strawberries and pineapple don't work.

4 tablespoons (½ stick) unsalted butter

2 cups sugar

1 cup all-purpose flour

1 cup buttermilk

1 teaspoon baking powder

½ teaspoon salt

½ teaspoon ground cinnamon

Pinch of grated nutmeg

3 cups fresh fruit, sliced peaches or nectarines, sliced peeled pears or
   apples, cranberries, or pitted cherries (see Note)

Whipped cream or ice cream (optional)

1. Heat the oven to 350°F. Put the butter in a 9 × 9-inch baking pan and place in the oven just until melted. Let cool to room temperature.

2. Combine 1 cup of the sugar, the flour, buttermilk, baking powder, salt, cinnamon, and nutmeg in a large bowl and mix just until smooth. Toss the fruit with the remaining 1 cup of sugar in a separate bowl. Pour the batter into the pan and tilt the pan to make an even layer. Arrange the fruit evenly over the batter and drizzle with the juices in the bowl.

3. Bake until the top of the cake is golden brown, about 1 hour 15 minutes. Serve warm, topped with whipped cream or ice cream, if desired.

Note: You may substitute 1 cup of rinsed blueberries or blackberries for an equal amount of the other fruit you are using, but using only those berries would make the cobbler soggy.

Pumpkin Pound Cake

Makes 12 servings

This cake has a nice spicy finish, and it stays moist for days. Serve it as is with a dusting of confectioners' sugar or toasted, with vanilla or butter pecan ice cream.

3 cups all-purpose flour

2 tablespoons baking powder

1 tablespoon pumpkin pie spice (see Note)

¼ teaspoon kosher salt

½ pound (2 sticks) unsalted butter, at room temperature

1½ cups sugar

1 teaspoon vanilla extract

One 16-ounce can solid pack pumpkin

5 large eggs

1. Heat the oven to 350°F. Butter and flour a 10-inch (12-cup) Bundt pan. Or use a nonstick Bundt pan.

2. Sift the flour, baking powder, pumpkin pie spice, and salt into a small bowl and set aside.

3. Cream the butter and sugar with an electric stand or handheld mixer, until light in color. Beat in the vanilla. Add the pumpkin gradually while beating on low speed. Add the eggs, one at a time, beating well after each. Fold the dry ingredients into the pumpkin mixture with a rubber spatula, making sure to scrape the sides of the bowl. Transfer the mixture to the pan and rap the pan on the counter once or twice to settle the batter.

4. Bake until it is golden brown on top and a cake tester or wooden pick inserted into the center comes out clean, about 1 hour. Let the cake cool in the pan about 30 minutes, then invert it onto a serving plate as described on page 241. Cool completely before slicing. *The cake can be stored, tightly wrapped or in a tightly sealed container, for up to 3 days.*

Note: If you can't find pumpkin pie spice, substitute a mixture of 1 teaspoon ground ginger, ½ teaspoon ground allspice, ½ teaspoon ground cinnamon, and ¼ teaspoon ground nutmeg. You can play around with these proportions, even adding a little freshly ground black pepper if you like.

Fold 1 cup chopped pecans or fresh or thawed frozen cranberries into the batter at the end of Step 3.

Cranberry Crunch Loaf

Makes 8 to 10 servings

Slices of this quick bread go on all our dessert platters. They're a green room favorite at the Joan Rivers and Geraldo Rivera television shows.

3 cups all-purpose flour

1½ teaspoons baking powder

½ teaspoon kosher salt

12 tablespoons (1½ sticks) unsalted butter, at room temperature

1¼ cups sugar

3 extra-large eggs

1½ teaspoons vanilla extract

⅔ cup buttermilk

1 cup cranberries, fresh or frozen (see Note)

Crumb Topping (recipe follows)

1. Heat the oven to 350°F. Butter and flour a 9 × 5-inch loaf pan.

2. Sift the flour, baking powder, and salt into a small bowl. Beat the butter with an electric stand or handheld mixer until creamy. Gradually beat in the sugar until the mixture is light and fluffy. Add the eggs, one at a time, beating well after each. Beat in the vanilla. Using a rubber spatula, fold in about a third of the flour, being sure to scrape the sides of the bowl. Fold in about a third of the buttermilk. Repeat twice with the remaining flour and buttermilk. Fold in the cranberries. Transfer the batter to the pan and smooth the top. Sprinkle the topping evenly over the top of the cake.

3. Bake until the topping is deep golden brown and a cake tester or wooden pick inserted into the center of the cake comes out clean, about 1 hour 30 minutes. Cool the cake in the pan, preferably on a wire rack, for 30 minutes. Carefully slide the cake from the pan and continue to cool at room temperature. *The cake may be stored, tightly wrapped or in a tightly sealed container, for up to 2 days.*

Note: If you use frozen cranberries, be sure they are completely thawed before adding them to the batter.

For a breakfast cake, substitute blueberries for the cranberries and omit the topping.

Use the batter for cranberry or blueberry muffins, with or without the crumb topping.

Makes 2 loosely packed cups

4 tablespoons (½ stick) unsalted butter, at room temperature

½ cup finely chopped pecans

½ cup (packed) light brown sugar

½ cup all-purpose flour

Combine the butter, pecans, brown sugar, and flour in a small bowl. Mix with your fingertips just until no pieces of butter remain. The topping should have the consistency of lumpy moist sand. Set aside.

Desserts

Raisin-Walnut Coffee Cake

Makes 8 servings

Yes, we do breakfast at Blue Collar Foods. We cater corporate breakfast meetings (prayer meetings, as some call them), and we sell breakfast goodies to coffee shops and espresso bars around Manhattan. This cake is part of just about every breakfast order we fill. It's that good. The recipe is unorthodox, but it's never let us down. Baking soda is sprinkled over the water used to soften dried fruit. We don't have a clue as to why it's done that way, but we say, "If it ain't broke, don't fix it."

¾ cup raisins

1½ cups water

3 cups sifted all-purpose flour

2 cups sugar

¾ cup vegetable oil

2 large eggs, beaten well

3 teaspoons vanilla extract

¾ cup chopped walnuts

1½ teaspoons baking soda

Confectioners' sugar, for dusting

1. Set the oven rack in the center position and heat the oven to 350°F. Grease and flour a 9-inch (12-cup) tube pan or two 9-inch loaf pans.

2. Place the raisins in a heatproof bowl. Bring the water to a boil and pour it over the raisins. Let stand until cool. In a large bowl, combine the flour, sugar, oil, eggs, and vanilla and beat until blended. Stir in the walnuts. When the raisin water is cool, sprinkle the baking soda over the surface and allow it to foam. Stir it into the batter. Pour the batter into the pan, rap it sharply on a hard surface two or three times, and place it in the oven.

3. Bake until a cake tester or wooden pick inserted in the center of the cake comes out clean, about 1 hour. Cool the cake in the pan 10 minutes. Invert it onto a serving platter. Let the cake cool completely. Sprinkle with confectioners' sugar before serving. *The cake may be prepared up to 2 days in advance. Store in an airtight container or wrapped in plastic wrap.*

Note: To invert the cake, run a table knife between the cake and the pan to loosen. Choose a plate a couple of inches larger than the cake pan. Place the plate on top of the pan and quickly turn the pan over. Hold in place until the cake slips from the pan onto the plate. Remove the pan.

Date Nut Bread

Makes 2 loaves

Blue Collar Food has grown and changed in ways we never anticipated. When a writer for _New York_ magazine asked us for some nostalgic sandwich recipes, we thought right away of cream cheese on date nut. That simple idea was the cornerstone of our wholesale business. We got a recipe from Bill's mother-in-law and fooled around with it until we got a sandwich more like the one Chris's mother used to put in his school lunch. People say our sandwich reminds them of the ones served for years at Chock Full o'Nuts coffee shops—high praise indeed.

> 4 cups (loosely packed) chopped pitted dates
> 2 teaspoons baking soda
> 1¼ cups water
> ¾ cup molasses
> 2 extra-large eggs, well beaten
> 2 teaspoons vanilla extract
> 4 cups all-purpose flour
> 1½ cups sugar
> 2 teaspoons baking powder
> 1 cup chopped walnuts

1. Place the dates in a large heatproof bowl and sprinkle them with the baking soda. Combine the water and molasses in a small saucepan and bring just to a boil. Pour over the dates. The baking soda will cause the mixture to foam. Let stand until cool.

2. Heat the oven to 350°F. Lightly grease two 9 × 5-inch loaf pans with vegetable spray or oil.

3. Beat the eggs into the date mixture with a fork until completely incorporated. Beat in the vanilla. Combine the flour, sugar, and baking powder in a separate bowl and stir to blend. Stir the flour mixture into the date mixture just until the dry ingredients are incorporated. Add the walnuts and continue mixing just until the walnuts are evenly distributed. Do not overwork the batter. Divide the batter between the pans.

4. Bake until the bread begins to pull away from the sides of the pan and a cake tester or wooden pick inserted into the center of the bread comes out clean, about 1 hour. Cool the loaves in the pan for 30 minutes. Remove from the pans and cool completely to room temperature. *The loaves may be stored, tightly wrapped, for up to 4 days or frozen for longer storage.*

Cheesecake, Plain and Fancy

Makes 8 servings

Desserts don't get much better than this. The cheesecake is creamy but light, and very easy to make. It has to be done ahead—actually an advantage for a party dessert. You might want to garnish the plain version with fresh berries or other fruit. Use your favorite recipe for a graham cracker or cookie crust or buy one. Keep your eye on the goal, which is to make the cheesecake. A storebought crust won't spoil it.

20 ounces cream cheese, at room temperature

1 cup sugar

4 extra-large eggs

1 tablespoon vanilla extract

One 9-inch graham cracker crust, homemade or store-bought

1.   Heat the oven to 350°F.

2.   Combine the cream cheese and sugar in a mixing bowl and beat with an electric mixer until light and fluffy, about 4 minutes. Add the eggs, one at a time, beating well after each addition. Add the vanilla and beat for 4 minutes. Pour the mixture into the crust.

3.   Bake until the edges are very lightly browned and the center is set, about 45 minutes. Remove from the oven and let cool to room temperature. Refrigerate until thoroughly chilled before serving. *The cheesecake may be prepared up to 1 day in advance and refrigerated.*

Variations

Raspberry Cheesecake: Sprinkle 1 cup of frozen raspberries over the graham cracker crust before pouring in the batter.

Mocha Chip Cheesecake: Dissolve 1 tablespoon instant coffee in 1 tablespoon coffee liqueur or coffee. Substitute this mixture for the vanilla extract. Sprinkle ½ cup chocolate chips over the crust before pouring in the batter.

Chocolate Cheesecake: Melt 6 ounces semisweet chocolate and add to the cream cheese mixture after the eggs.

Apple Crumb Pie

Makes 8 servings

This is a great pie for a party because you can make the filling, topping, and crust ahead (or buy one). Combine them and bake the pie at the last minute.

2 tablespoons unsalted butter

3 pounds pie apples, such as Rome or Cortland, peeled, cored, and sliced ¼ inch thick (about 6 cups)

½ cup granulated sugar

½ cup (packed) light brown sugar

½ teaspoon ground cinnamon

Pinch of grated nutmeg

Pinch of ground cloves

1 tablespoon cornstarch

¼ cup apple cider or apple juice

One 9-inch pie shell, homemade or store-bought (See Note)

Crumb Topping (page 239)

1. Melt the butter in a large skillet over medium-low heat. Add the apples, the granulated and the brown sugar, the cinnamon, nutmeg, and cloves. Cook, stirring to dissolve the sugar, until the apples begin to release their juices. Dissolve the cornstarch into the cider and stir into the apples. Heat to simmering and stir constantly until thickened, 2 to 3 minutes. Cool the apple filling to room temperature.

2. Heat the oven to 350°F.

3. Transfer the filling to the pie shell and smooth the top. Crumble the topping evenly over the filling.

4. Bake until the crust and topping are golden brown and the filling is bubbling, about 50 minutes. Cool to lukewarm or room temperature before serving.

Note: A word about pie crusts. We buy pie crusts from a bakery supply house and keep them on hand in the freezer for emergency desserts and quiches. A few minutes at room temperature and the shells are ready to fill or prebake. If you have a favorite pie shell recipe, and feel like making it, use that in any of the recipes that call for a store-bought shell.

Peach and Blueberry Pie

Makes 8 servings

This pie is bursting with the flavors of summer. You can use two store-bought pie shells, one for the bottom and one for the top.

4 large ripe peaches, peeled, pitted, and thinly sliced (about 4 cups)

1½ cups fresh blueberries, rinsed and well drained

1 cup sugar

2 tablespoons cornstarch

2 teaspoons vanilla extract

½ teaspoon ground cinnamon

Two 9-inch pie shells, homemade or store-bought

1 egg, well beaten with a few drops of water (optional)

Sugar, for glazing crust (optional)

1. Place a baking sheet or two sheets of aluminum foil on the bottom of the oven to catch any juices from the pie. Heat the oven to 350°F.

2. Combine the peaches, blueberries, sugar, cornstarch, vanilla, and cinnamon in a large mixing bowl. Stir lightly with a rubber spatula until the cornstarch is dissolved and the fruit is coated with syrup. Pour the filling into one of the pie shells and invert the second shell over the filling. Crimp the edges together to seal in the filling and press around the edge of the pie plate with a fork. Poke several holes in the top crust with a small knife to allow the steam to escape during baking.

3. Bake until golden brown and bubbling, about 1 hour. Brush the pie with beaten egg and sprinkle with sugar for the last 15 minutes of baking, if desired. Let cool to room temperature before serving.

Pecan Pie Gone Haywire

Makes 8 servings

People go a bit crazy too when they taste this incredible pie.

8 tablespoons (1 stick) unsalted butter, at room temperature

¾ cup sugar

3 eggs

½ cup honey

1 teaspoon vanilla extract or dark rum

¾ cup chopped pecans

½ cup shredded sweetened coconut

1 cup semisweet chocolate chips

One 9-inch pie shell, homemade or store-bought

1. Heat the oven to 350°F.

2. Cream the butter and sugar in a medium bowl with an electric mixer until light and fluffy. Add the eggs, one at a time, beating well and scraping down the sides of the bowl after each addition. Slowly beat in the honey. Beat in the vanilla. Combine the pecans, coconut, and chocolate chips in a small bowl and toss to mix. Spread this mixture over the bottom of the pie shell. Pour the egg mixture into the shell and smooth the top.

3. Bake until the crust is golden brown around the edges and the filling is set in the center, about 45 minutes. Cool completely to room temperature before serving. *The pie may be prepared completely up to 1 day in advance. Cover and store in a cool place.*

Desserts

Butterscotch Meringue Pie

Makes 8 servings

Bill has been carrying this recipe in his culinary kit bag ever since his first restaurant job in North Carolina at age fourteen. He's refined and adapted it over the years while keeping it simple. This is another good party pie since you can prepare the filling and fill the shell a day ahead, then do the meringue as late as fifteen minutes before serving.

3 cups milk

½ cup all-purpose flour

1 cup (packed) dark brown sugar

1 tablespoon vanilla extract

3 large eggs, separated

One 9-inch pie shell, homemade or store-bought, baked

1 tablespoon granulated sugar

1. Combine the milk, flour, brown sugar, and vanilla in a mixing bowl and beat with a whisk or electric mixer until the mixture is well blended and no lumps remain. Transfer the mixture to a medium saucepan and place over medium-high heat. Stir constantly with a wooden spoon, paying special attention to the sides and bottom of the pan, until the mixture comes to a boil. Reduce the heat and simmer, stirring, for 2 minutes. Pour back into the bowl and whisk in the egg yolks, one at a time. Strain the filling into the pie shell and let it cool completely to room temperature. *The pie may be made to this point up to 1 day in advance. Refrigerate the pie and the egg whites separately until ready to finish the pie.*

2. Heat the oven to 350°F.

3. Beat the egg whites in a medium bowl with a whisk or electric mixer until foamy. Add the granulated sugar and continue beating until stiff and shiny. Spread the meringue completely over the pie filling, mounding it in the middle.

4. Bake just until the top of the meringue is golden brown, about 5 minutes. Let stand 5 to 10 minutes or up to several hours before serving.

Blue Collar Brownies

Makes twenty-four 2-inch brownies

It's almost impossible to keep brownies on hand even though we bake them by the hundreds. They are incredibly popular. Fortunately, they freeze well, so we try to get a few batches ahead when we have a quiet moment, which——we're not complaining——is rare.

14 ounces good-quality semisweet chocolate (see Note)

1 cup sugar

12 tablespoons (1½ sticks) unsalted butter

1 cup all-purpose flour

2 teaspoons baking powder

¼ teaspoon kosher salt

4 large eggs

2 tablespoons instant coffee

1 tablespoon vanilla extract

1½ cups chopped walnuts

1.   Melt the chocolate, sugar, and butter in the top of a double boiler. Stir occasionally until the chocolate is melted and the mixture is smooth, about 10 minutes. Make sure the water stays at a bare simmer; if it gets too hot the chocolate will separate. Let cool to room temperature.

2.   Heat the oven to 350°F. Lightly butter and flour a 13 × 9-inch baking pan.

3.   Sift the flour, baking powder, and salt into a bowl and set aside.

4. Beat the eggs, coffee, and vanilla in a separate bowl until foamy. Beat this mixture into the chocolate mixture until smooth. Fold in the flour just until no streaks of white remain. Fold in the walnuts. Pour the batter into the pan and smooth into an even layer.

5. Bake until the edges are crisp and begin to pull away from the pan and the top is set, about 30 minutes. (The center of the brownies will still be slightly soft to the touch and a toothpick or cake tester inserted in the center will not come out clean.) Let cool completely. Cut the brownies into 2-inch squares. This is easier if the brownies are chilled in the pan for 10 to 20 minutes first. *The brownies may be made up to 2 days in advance and refrigerated, covered. Bring to room temperature before serving. The brownies may also be frozen, well wrapped in aluminum foil.*

Notes: Use imported chocolate with a high percentage of cocoa butter, such as Callebaut, Guittard, or Lindt.

If you don't have a double boiler, you may use a microwave oven. Melt the butter according to manufacturer's directions.

Our Chocolate Cake

Makes 8 servings

After a long affair with the densest and most decadent of chocolate desserts, we discovered that the chocolate cake we, and many of our customers, prefer is this one. It's more like the Girl Next Door than the Lady in Red. You can have it as is with a glass of milk or iced with your favorite frosting. If you're in the mood to gild the lily, fill and frost the cake with Blue Collar Chocolate Mousse.

2 cups all-purpose flour

⅔ cup cocoa powder (see Note)

1 teaspoon baking soda

1 teaspoon baking powder

1 teaspoon kosher salt

12 tablespoons (1½ sticks) unsalted butter, at room temperature

1½ cups sugar

3 large eggs

1½ teaspoons vanilla extract or rum

1½ cups buttermilk

1. Heat the oven to 350°F. Lightly butter and flour a 13 × 9-inch baking pan.

2. Sift the flour, cocoa, baking soda, baking powder, and salt into a bowl. Beat the butter with an electric stand or handheld mixer until creamy. Gradually beat in the sugar until the mixture is light and fluffy. Add the eggs, one at a time, beating well after each. Beat in the vanilla. Fold in about a third of the dry ingredients, making sure to scrape the sides of the bowl. Fold in half the buttermilk. Repeat with half the remaining dry ingredients and all the remaining buttermilk. Fold in the remaining dry ingredients. Transfer the batter to the pan.

3. Bake until the cake springs back when touched and a cake tester or wooden pick inserted into the center comes out clean. Cool the cake completely in the pan. Cut into eight 4½ × 3-inch pieces.

Note: Don't be tempted to use imported Dutch process or Hershey's European style cocoa for this cake. A good-quality nonalkalized cocoa is what you need.

Can something this rich, this elegant be *Blue Collar*? Absolutely, when it's this simple to make. Since it must be made ahead, it's the perfect dessert for a dinner with chocolate-loving friends.

10 ounces good-quality semisweet or extra bittersweet chocolate (see Note)

2 tablespoons unsalted butter

4 large eggs, separated

1 cup heavy cream, very cold

1 tablespoon coffee liqueur, such as Tia Maria or Kahlúa, or 1 teaspoon vanilla extract

Whipped cream (optional)

Fresh berries (optional)

1. Break up or chop the chocolate into small chunks. Melt the chocolate and butter in the top of a double boiler or improvise one as described on page 252. Stir occasionally until the chocolate is completely melted, about 10 minutes. Keep the water at a bare simmer. Remove from the heat and beat in the egg yolks, one at a time. Beat the egg whites in a separate bowl with an electric mixer just until they hold soft peaks. Fold the egg whites into the chocolate mixture, half at a time, using a rubber spatula. Fold gently, making sure to scrape the bottom and sides of the bowl. Stop folding when the whites have been half incorporated into the chocolate. Whip the cream with an electric mixer just until it holds soft peaks. Add the liqueur to the chocolate mixture. Fold in the whipped cream just until no white streaks remain.

2. Transfer the mousse to a serving bowl or individual dishes and refrigerate until completely set, at least 3 hours or up to 1 day. Serve with whipped cream and/or fresh berries, if desired.

Note: For this dessert, it's essential to use the best chocolate you can afford, one with a high percentage of cocoa butter, such as Callebaut, Guittard, or Pernigotti.

Chocolate Pudding

Makes 6 servings

If you grew up on My *T *Fine, you don't know how fine chocolate pudding can be——and how simple it is to make it from scratch. Fifteen minutes from start to finish, not much longer than cooking the packaged stuff. We offer this occasionally to our corporate and photographer clients. They get a kick out of it.

6 ounces good-quality semisweet chocolate (see Note)

3 cups milk

1 cup heavy cream

1 cup sugar

½ cup all-purpose flour

1 teaspoon vanilla extract

3 large egg yolks

Whipped cream, for garnish (optional)

Mint leaves, for garnish (optional)

1. Place the chocolate in a small heatproof bowl in the oven, turned to the lowest setting. Check often, stirring each time. Keep the melted chocolate in a warm place to prevent it from turning solid.

2. Combine the milk, cream, sugar, flour, and vanilla in a mixing bowl. Beat with a wire whisk until the flour and sugar are dissolved. Pour the mixture into a medium saucepan and place over medium heat. Cook, stirring constantly, until the mixture begins to boil. Adjust the heat to a slow boil and cook until the mixture is thickened, about 2 minutes. Stir constantly, paying special attention to the bottom and corners of the pan. Pour the mixture through a fine strainer into a heatproof bowl. Add the egg yolks one at a time, whisking well after each. Fold in the chocolate until completely incorporated.

3. Divide the mixture among 6 serving cups. Apply a piece of plastic wrap directly on the surface of each to prevent a skin from forming. Refrigerate until ready to serve, up to 2 days. Garnish with whipped cream and fresh mint, if desired.

Berries with Balsamic Vinegar and Mint

Makes 4 servings

The idea of dressing berries with balsamic vinegar may seem very novel, not to say nouvelle, but it is actually a historic combination. We add a fillip of mint.

- 1 pint fresh strawberries
- 1 pint fresh blueberries
- 1 tablespoon sugar
- 1 teaspoon balsamic vinegar
- 8 to 10 mint leaves, torn into small pieces

Cut the stems from the strawberries. Rinse them and the blueberries very briefly under cold water and drain well on paper towels. Combine the berries in a bowl and sprinkle them with the sugar. Let stand at room temperature until the sugar is dissolved, about 30 minutes. Just before serving add the vinegar and mint leaves to the bowl and toss to coat the berries.

We were looking for a shortcake to put our signature to when we came up with the idea of making the dough for Aunt Elsie's Plum Cake with brown sugar. It's a moist but not too sweet biscuit-style shortcake. We also found an unusual way to macerate the berries, inspired in part by a recipe for Berry Shortcake that friend Helen Witty developed years ago. If you don't have an eight-inch cake pan, you can pat the dough out into a rough eight-inch circle of even thickness and bake it on a cookie sheet.

Rich Pastry Dough (page 233), made with light brown sugar instead of
     granulated sugar

2 tablespoons sugar

1 tablespoon orange juice

1 tablespoon seedless raspberry preserves

4 cups assorted berries, including hulled strawberries, raspberries,
     blueberries, and/or blackberries

1½ cups heavy cream, whipped

1.   Heat the oven to 350°F.

2.   Make the dough and place into an 8-inch round nonstick or lightly greased cake pan. Pat the dough to an even thickness. Lightly score the top to mark 6 even wedges. Bake until golden brown and a cake tester or wooden pick inserted into the center comes out clean, about 25 minutes. *The shortbread can be made up to several hours in advance. Store, loosely covered, at room temperature.*

3. About 1 hour before serving, combine the sugar, orange juice, and raspberry preserves in a medium mixing bowl. Stir until the sugar is dissolved. Slice the strawberries if you are using them, and place them along with the other berries in the bowl. Toss gently until the berries are coated. Let the berries stand, tossing once or twice, for 30 minutes to 1 hour.

4. To serve the shortcake whole, split it into top and bottom halves with a serrated knife. Place the bottom on a serving platter and spoon the berries over it. Drizzle the juices from the bowl over the berries. Top the berries with some of the whipped cream and place the top of the shortcake over the whipped cream. Cut through the wedges to serve. For individual servings, cut the cake into wedges following the marks on top of the cake. Split each wedge with a serrated knife or your fingers. Place the bottoms on serving plates and, top with berries, juice, and a dollop of whipped cream. Place the top off center over the whipped cream. Either way, serve at once, passing the remaining whipped cream.

This light dessert is a good choice for holiday entertaining. The burgundy-colored pears look spectacular served on a puddle of Custard Sauce. A few peppercorns in the poaching liquid add a note of mystery.

One 750-ml bottle good-quality Chianti wine

3 cups water

2 cups sugar

1 lemon

1 orange

10 black peppercorns

4 whole cloves

½ cinnamon stick (2-inch piece)

4 ripe but firm Bartlett pears (see Note)

Custard Sauce (recipe follows)

1. Combine the wine, water, and sugar in a large nonreactive saucepan. Peel the zest from the lemon and orange, being careful to remove only the thin outer yellow or orange layer without the white pith. Add the zests to the pan. Cut a 4-inch square of double-thick cheesecloth and place the peppercorns, cloves, and cinnamon in the center. Tie securely with kitchen twine. Heat the wine mixture to a simmer over medium heat and stir until the sugar is dissolved. Add the spice bundle, reduce the heat, and simmer, covered, for 15 minutes. Prepare the pears: Peel them with a vegetable peeler, leaving the stems intact. Using an apple corer or small knife, cut out the cores and seeds from the bottom, leaving the pears whole and not cutting through the sides.

2. Add the pears. There should be enough liquid to cover the pears; if not, transfer to a different pan. Poach the pears, turning them gently from time to time, until tender but not mushy, about 15 to 25 minutes, depending on how ripe they are. Test for doneness with a long wooden skewer or cake tester. Remove the pan from the heat and let the pears cool in the syrup. *The pears can be prepared to this point up to 2 days in advance and refrigerated in their cooking liquid.*

3. Refrigerate the pears until chilled and firm, then remove them from the liquid. Serve at room temperature or slightly warmed with Custard Sauce. Strain and reserve the poaching liquid for rewarming the pears or for poaching more pears. *The liquid will keep, tightly covered, in the refrigerator for up to 3 weeks.*

Note: Pears are usually sold unripe. Let them ripen to the point where they are still firm but have a faint pear aroma. Bartlett, Bosc, and Anjou are the best varieties for poaching.

Custard Sauce

Makes 2 cups

Very simple to prepare, especially after the first one or two times, custard sauce (also known on restaurant menus as Crème Anglaise) can be a secret weapon in your dessert arsenal. Use it to jazz up desserts from sliced fresh fruit to chocolate cake to fruit tarts. Also, it holds perfectly in the refrigerator up to 3 days. You can vary the flavor by replacing the vanilla extract with the flavored liqueur of your choice.

4 large egg yolks
2 cups milk
½ cup sugar
1 teaspoon vanilla extract

1. Place the egg yolks in a small heatproof bowl. Combine the milk, sugar, and vanilla in a small nonreactive saucepan. Heat over medium heat, stirring, until the sugar is dissolved and the milk just begins to simmer. Whisk the yolks lightly to break them up. Remove the pan from the heat and slowly ladle about half the hot milk into the yolks while whisking. (Place a damp kitchen towel under the bowl to help hold it steady, thus freeing both your hands for this task.) Be sure to add the milk slowly and to whisk along the bottom and sides of the bowl to mix all the yolks into the milk. Return the pan to the heat and stir in the egg mixture. Stir constantly with a wooden spoon, paying careful attention to the bottom and corners of the pan, until some steam rises from the surface and the custard is thickened enough to lightly coat a metal spoon (180° to 182°F. on an instant-reading thermometer).

2. Immediately strain the custard into a bowl. Stir occasionally as it cools to room temperature. Place a piece of plastic wrap directly on the surface to prevent a skin from forming. *The sauce may be refrigerated for up to 3 days.*

Like many of our recipes, this one has evolved over the years we've worked together. Originally we used caramelized sugar as a sweetener, but then we remembered how great maple syrup is with pears, peaches, even bananas. Be sure to let the pudding stand a good long time to guarantee it puffs up when baked.

20 slices day-old good-quality white bread

8 tablespoons (1 stick) unsalted butter, at room temperature

3 cups milk

1 cup maple syrup

⅓ cup (packed) light or dark brown sugar

6 large eggs

5 ripe Bosc pears or ripe peaches, peeled, pitted, and sliced, or 3 large
      ripe bananas, peeled and sliced (about 3 cups)

½ teaspoon ground cinnamon

1. Spread both sides of the bread slices lightly with 6 tablespoons of the butter and set aside.

2. Combine the milk, maple syrup, and brown sugar in a small saucepan. Stir over low heat until the sugar is dissolved. Beat the eggs in a medium bowl until well blended. Slowly stir in the warm maple syrup mixture.

3. Lightly butter a 13 × 9-inch baking pan. Arrange 6 of the bread slices over the bottom of the dish. Top with half of the fruit. Pour a third of the custard mixture over the fruit. Repeat with 6 more slices of bread, the remaining fruit, and half the remaining custard. Arrange the last 8 slices of bread, overlapping, on top of the fruit. Pour the remaining custard over the bread and press the bread lightly so it absorbs the custard. Sprinkle the top with cinnamon. Let the pudding stand in a

(continued)

Desserts

265

cool place for 30 to 45 minutes before baking. *The pudding may be prepared to this point up to 6 hours in advance and refrigerated, tightly covered. Let stand at room temperature for 30 minutes before baking.*

4. Heat the oven to 350°F.

5. Bake the pudding until the top is golden brown and firm. To be sure the custard is set, poke the center with a knife and make sure it is not runny. Remove the bread pudding and let cool for 15 to 45 minutes before serving. *The pudding may be baked up to 1 day before serving. Once cool, refrigerate the pudding. Rewarm it in the dish in an oven set to the lowest setting before serving.*

Index

Index

271